Property and Trust Law in Finland

Property and Trust Law in Finland

Erkki J. Hollo

This book was originally published as a monograph in the International Encyclopaedia of Laws/Property and Trust Law.

General Editor: Roger Blanpain
Associate General Editor: Michele Colucci
Volume Editors: Alain Verbeke, Vincent Sagaert

Wolters Kluwer
Law & Business

Published by:
Kluwer Law International
PO Box 316
2400 AH Alphen aan den Rijn
The Netherlands
Website: www.kluwerlaw.com

Sold and distributed in North, Central and South America by:
Aspen Publishers, Inc.
7201 McKinney Circle
Frederick, MD 21704
United States of America
Email: customer.service@aspenpublishers.com

Sold and distributed in all other countries by:
Turpin Distribution Services Ltd.
Stratton Business Park
Pegasus Drive, Biggleswade
Bedfordshire SG18 8TQ
United Kingdom
Email: kluwerlaw@turpin-distribution.com

Printed on acid-free paper.

ISBN 978-90-411-4726-4

This title is available on www.kluwerlawonline.com

Printed and Bound by CPI Group (UK) Ltd, Croydon, CR0 4YY.

The Author

The author, professor Dr.Dr.iur. (Helsinki and Tübingen) Erkki J. Hollo, Faculty of Law, University of Helsinki, was appointed in 1997 full professor of land property and environmental law at this Faculty, emeritus 2008. Before that he was professor of economic law at the Helsinki University of Technology since 1977 and since 1983, for eight years, member and Justice of the Finnish Supreme Administrative Court. One of his theses treated comparative private law, especially law of contracts, the other issues dealing with water property rights and pollution.

He is *inter alia* a board member of the Finnish Academy of Sciences, president of honour of the European Council for Agricultural Law (CEDR) and member of the International Union of Nature Conservation (IUCN) Law Commission. He has participated in numerous governmental law commissions, most of them dealing with natural resources, liability issues and environmental protection. He has also conducted approximation studies for accession states to the European Union.

He has published 30 books and about 250 articles, mainly in land property, environmental and water law as well as comparative law. The numerous research projects include topics on property law, water law, law on biotechnology and environmental administration as well as court procedures.

The Author

Table of Contents

Table of Contents

Preliminary Note

First Edition:

This monograph gives a brief overview of the Finnish law on property rights. For real property, the presentation covers the basic concepts and institutions as well as the registration system, the establishment of property rights and the security order. Also categories of limited rights, especially lease and casements, are covered. As far as movable property is concerned the overview presents corresponding concepts and regulatory systems.

The presentation of legislation and legal practice has been taken into account up to autumn 2007. For the proof of English language, my thanks go to Mr David Davies for his valuable corrections and comments.

Second Edition:

For the second edition, the content has been updated and also some minor amendments are made. Legal sources are reviewed up to the end of 2011.

List of Abbreviations

CAP	(EU) Common Agricultural Policy
ComC	Commercial Code
EU	European Union
HerC	Heritage Code
KHO	(Decisions of the) Supreme Administrative Court
KKO	(Decisions of the) Supreme Court
LUBA	Act on Land Use and Building
REC	Real Estate Code
REFA	Real Estate Formation Act
UPOV	International Union for the Protection of New Varieties of Plants
WIPO	World Intellectual Property Organization
WTO	World Trade Organization

List of Abbreviations

General Introduction

Chapter 1. General Information of the Country

§1. Geography and Population

1. Finland is situated in Northern Europe and is part of the geographical and cultural area of Scandinavia. The location is between 60 and 70 degrees northern latitude, which is equal to a distance in the north-south direction of about 1,000 kilometres. The south-western part of the country extends from the Finnish Gulf in the south to the Gulf of Bothnia in the west, both bays of the Baltic Sea. The remaining part of the country has borders on land or in rivers with Sweden to the west, Norway to the north, and Russia to the east. The State covers an area of 338,000 km^2, of which 9% are inland watercourses, among them approximately 60,000 lakes. Forest land (mainly pine and spruce) exceeds 60% of the area, marshland about 30%, and cultivated land (primarily barley and oats) 6%. The main cities are located in the southern part of the country: Helsinki (the capital, with 550,000 inhabitants), Espoo, Vantaa, Turku and Tampere. The main city in the northern region is Oulu.

2. The largest part of the population lives in the southern half of the country. The population in 2010 was 5.4 million inhabitants, which gives a population density of only seventeen inhabitants per square kilometre. The annual growth rate is 0.3%. Thus, basically due to geographical conditions, Finland is the country with the lowest population density in the European Union. Life expectancy for men is 76.7 and for women 82.3 years. The average age of men was 40.0 and women 42.3 years. As in other European countries, Finland's demographic pyramid is dominated by middle-aged population groups. The average household size is 2.2 persons, of whom 54% live in single-family houses and 46% in apartment blocks. One-fifth of the population lives within the metropolitan area of Helsinki, and roughly 84% of the population lives in urban areas. This makes the settlement density in rural areas rather low. A high amount of countryside habitation is composed of holiday cottages.

§2. Cultural and Social Situation

I. History

3. Culturally and legally, Finland belongs to the tradition of Central and Western Europe. The impact of changing historical conditions in the Baltic Sea region has been and continues to be a major factor. The entrance to Central Europe was supported during the centuries by the partnership with the Swedish Kingdom until 1809. After that, Finland was separated and became an autonomous Grand Duchy within the Russian Empire until its independence in 1917. During the nineteenth century, Finland maintained intensive cultural and economic relations with the States on the continent, especially with Germany and France, as well as traditionally with the Scandinavian countries. Swedish used to be the official language, but as a result of arising nationalism, the Finnish language acquired official status by the middle of the nineteenth century. After that, the Finnish language became more and more dominant, but the country still has two official languages, with the number of native Swedish-speaking people today around 5.5%.

II. Society

4. Finland has two official (State) religions: Lutheran,78% and Orthodox, 1%. Accordingly, these two religious communities are of public law, and other churches are organized as associations of private law. As far as the level of education is concerned, over 33% of the active population has a school degree; this is said to be the highest rate within the European Union. Three-quarters of households are connected to personal computers, and 70% have an Internet connection. The number of mobile phones covers 97% of the households. The unemployment rate is approximately 7.8% (2011). The average monthly income in 2006 was EUR 3,240 for men and EUR 2,640 for women.

5. After World War II, Finland lost a large area in the East (Carelia) to the Soviet Union, but the cultural and economic traditions with Europe were maintained. Trade with the Soviet Union played an important role, but due to its multi-faceted economic structure, Finland survived the intense changes in Eastern Europe at the beginning of the 1990s. Generally, the development in this decade favoured the efforts to participate in the traditional European context. For that reason, Finland decided to enter the European Union in 1995. It is also a member of the European Monetary Union (EMU).

6. Freedom of trade is constitutionally guaranteed and regulated in detail by the Act on Freedom of Trade (122/1919). Finnish and European companies as well as Finnish citizens may carry on trade while complying with good practice. Other than domestic trade, activities should be notified to the public trade register, which gives information about notifications of trade in relation to registered companies. Certain professional services which entail liability towards the public or clients may require a permit (e.g., loan office) or registration (e.g., estate agent).

7. The economic structure according to main employment branches is as follows: industry 19%, trade and tourism 16%, financial business services 14%, transport and communications 7%, construction 7%, and agriculture 4%. Foreign trade numbers for 2010 were EUR 52 million for exports and EUR 50.5 million for imports. Main export materials were electrical equipment (21.4%) and pulp-paper products (15.9%). The gross domestic product in 2010 was EUR 180 billion, EUR 31,900 per capita (nominal, adjusted EUR 27,800) in 2006.

III. Climate

8. The location in Northern Europe between Scandinavia and Russia dominates the climate, which is characterized by relatively cold winters and, due to the impact of the Gulf Stream, mild summers. For this reason, agriculture is prosperous only in the southern part of the country. Lately there have been rather remarkable variations of temperatures and rain. The long-term average temperature in Helsinki varies between 17 degrees centigrade in summer and minus 5 degrees in winter.

§3. Political System and State Powers

I. Parliament and Legislative Process

A. *Parliament*

9. The Finnish Parliament has 200 deputies in one chamber. The electoral period for the Parliament is four years, with close to ten political parties recently represented. After the elections of 2011 there are four parties with almost equal support and a number of minor ones. The three traditionally dominant parties are the Social Democratic Party, the Finnish Centre (formerly Agrarian Movement), and the right wing National Coalition, in 2011 joined by a competing nationalist party. Of these the National Coalition and the Social Democrats are currently serving as State Government this term (since 2011). Some smaller parties have a rather stable position in the Parliament. For example, the Swedish Party, the Green Party and the Left Alliance occasionally hold ministerial portfolios in the Government; presently the Swedish Party and the Greens hold these positions. The autonomous province of Åland has one permanent representative in the Parliament.

10. The Parliament works in committee and plenary sessions. Legislative committees are nominated for specific areas in society but some of the committees have a more general function rather than just a sectoral task. The committee for constitutional law considers cases where constitutional legislation may be necessary. This is the case when basic rights of citizens, including the protection of property rights, are involved or State security and similar interests are at stake. As a rule, the opinion of this committee is binding for the choice of legislative order in the Parliament itself. Other general committees to be mentioned are the committee for general law and the committee for law and economy. The Parliament is conducted by a chairman (speaker) and vice-chairmen, who form the council of chairmen, a body with interior competences in the Parliament.

B. Government

11. The party which gets the largest number of members in the Parliament at the general election is usually entitled to appoint the candidate for the office of prime minister. The election of this person will be confirmed by the Parliament, and the prime minister is nominated by the President of the Republic. The State Government, of which the prime minister is the head, is composed of ministers. These are chosen by the prime minister on the basis of political negotiations concerning the political programme of the Government. The President of the Republic nominates the selected ministers for each ministerial function. The members of the Government, called ministers, are as a rule heads of departments (ministries) of the State administration. The number and sectors of both ministries and ministers may vary, though the changes from one electoral period to another are not significant. Permanent ministries are the Ministry of Justice, the Ministry for Foreign Affairs, and the Ministry of Employment and the Economy. It is noteworthy that within the area of property law, there are also ministries for environment, agriculture and forestry, and internal affairs.[1]

C. President of the Republic

12. The President of the Republic is elected for a period of six years through direct elections, and re-election is possible only once. The powers of the President today are not as wide as they used to be before the Constitution of 2000. But still the President holds important duties, especially in the area of foreign affairs and national defence. Decisions within the competence of the President are made in the formal sessions of the State Government, i.e., in the presence of the ministers. Under certain conditions, the President has a right of veto.

D. Political Parties

13. The political system is based on democratic parliamentarism with a multi-party system. Finland became a sovereign State in 1917, but as early as 1906 when Finland was still an autonomous part of the Russian Empire, the one-chamber parliament was elected. Before that Finland had as legislator a national assembly based on representatives of estates, i.e., social classes. This assembly had the right to legislate on internal political matters during the period, which also was fruitful

1. Act on the State Council 175/2003.

for strengthening Finnish identity, including the language and the national monetary system.

14. The autonomous region of the Åland Islands has a different position with strict conditions regarding the right to regional residence. The transfer of agricultural land to others, other than farmers, used to be under State control, but this system does not exist any longer.[2]

2. See Act on right to acquire arable and forestry land 391/26.5.1978, abolished in 1997.

Chapter 2. Legal Background of the Country

§1. Legal Family and Tradition

15. Finnish Law has developed in accordance with the Scandinavian legal tradition, especially since Finland was for a long time a part of the Kingdom of Sweden. After this period, the legal structure adopted national differences, but the basic legal ideology remained the same. Scandinavian Law has its roots within the Continent, especially German law. However, property law has features of its own, especially in the system of conveyance and in the structure of real estate units. One can also find recent influences from Anglo-Saxon law in the area of economic regulations, for instance, leasing and securities. As a member of the European Union Finland has to transpose the entire legal system of the Union as well.

§2. Relation and Hierarchy between the Sources of Law

16. Finland adopted a constitutional reform in 2000. The previous Constitution of 1919 had been partly amended earlier. The present Constitution does not bring important changes to the system of constitutional rights or the rules of parliamentarism. Instead, the task has been to give the Constitution a more integrated function within the whole legal system because Finland has no explicit body or constitutional court to control the implementation of constitutional provisions. Courts, especially the two Supreme Courts, are supposed to take the constitutional provisions into account whenever these are at stake in a matter of appeal. Sometimes this may lead to a more modified interpretation of general legislation or previous practices. Another sector where the constitutional reform has brought changes is in the division of power between the Government and the President of the Republic, the latter of which has, to some extent, lost previous competences to the Government. The latest modifications of the legal power of the President entered into force 1 March 2012.

17. Sources of law are legislative acts, legal practice or jurisdiction, and, to some extent, customary law and legal principles. Other legal materials, such as official statements (*travaux préparatoires*) and valid doctrine (*herrschende Lehre*), may influence legal decision-making. Written law is decisive, and it consists of the Constitution (2000) itself, further constitutional acts, and common legislation of the Parliament. As a rule, the courts cannot overrule legislation in force. However, since the Constitution has a certain direct effect, constitutional provisions, especially those concerning basic rights, may give courts the power, case-by-case, to modify legislative practices if these are considered to be in conflict with the Constitution. Thus, the constitutional provisions may directly influence or modify the application of existing laws if they are not in accordance with the Constitution. In principle, however, the courts do not act as 'legislators' when a needed legislation does not exist at all, because, in principle, interpretations obviously *contra legem* should not be taken by courts or other authorities.

18. As far as civil rights are concerned, it is worthwhile again in this context to mention the basic property right (Constitution section 15), the freedom of trade, and the provision termed 'civil freedom right'. In addition, human rights are guaranteed by the Constitution. The human right aspect has indeed also been of some importance for property law in the light of international conventions. Essentially, the role of these provisions is to authorize and to oblige the Parliament to enact appropriate (general) legislation for the implementation of the provisions. It is, hence, a kind of self-commitment of the legislator to act. A further noteworthy constitutional provision is the environmental basic right (Constitution section 20). This ruling provides a general obligation on everyone to take liability for environmental damage. On the other hand, it stipulates a right for the public involved to participate in environmental decision-making; this includes, for instance, land-use planning.

§3. Jurisdiction and Judicial Process

19. Finland has a dual court system with general courts and administrative courts. Some specific tribunals and procedures for defined situations also exist. For example, this is the case in appeal matters concerning land survey and agriculture where there is in the first instance a (regional) land court and a (central) appeal body for rural industries. As a rule, cases related to land ownership and property rights fall within the mandate of the general courts; land-use management (planning, permits) is part of administrative jurisdiction.

20. As far as the court system is concerned, courts of general jurisdiction operate at three levels, whereas administrative courts have only two instances. The supreme jurisdiction is consequently shared by the Supreme Court and the Supreme Administrative Court. General courts at local level have an exclusive competence in civil and criminal law cases, with appeals in the first instance to the Regional Court of Appeal. Appeals to the Supreme Court require prior leave to appeal, which the court itself may grant under specific conditions. Administrative courts do not exist at the local level. Instead, administrative authorities in the State and municipal administration make their decisions, which are subject to appeal in the regional administrative courts. Due to the existence of just one level of appellate courts, there are as a rule in material cases only occasionally restrictions of appeal to the Supreme Administrative Court. This court is also competent to handle appeals against the decisions of the State Government and the ministries on legal grounds. Finland has no constitutional court. The constitutionality of legislation is decided by the Parliament in a specific hearing of its constitutional committee.

21. Procedural rules for jurisdiction and appeal are provided in law. For civil and criminal jurisdiction, the core legislation incorporates the Code of Jurisdiction (1734). In addition, there are legislative acts on the publicity of judicial proceedings, legal aid, and more. Arbitration as an alternative to jurisdiction is based on separate legislation (Arbitration Act 967/1992). Proceedings concerning execution are regulated separately as well by a specific Execution Code (705/2006). As far as administrative jurisdiction is concerned, corresponding rulings are based on the Administrative Jurisdiction Act (586/1996).

§4. Executive Powers and Administrative Law

22. Executive powers belong to the administrative authorities of the State and the municipalities. In civil and criminal law, there are executive authorities under the supervision of the Ministry of Justice. The public administration of the State is organized within the different ministries, which in many cases have a regional (district) administration. This is the case in matters dealing with land survey and the real estate register (Ministry of Agriculture and Forestry) as well as land-use planning and environmental legislation (Ministry of the Environment). Energy and mining issues are within the competence of the Ministry for Employment and the Economy. In cases where the legislation touches the competence of different sectors, the State Government may have the power to enact general guidelines and regulations (e.g., national land-use guidelines).

23. Administrative law is based on general legislation and administrative procedures of the Administration Act (434/2003). Due to the self-government of municipalities, there are some peculiarities concerning administrative decision-making in municipalities and their authorities (Municipalities Act 365/1995). Since State administration as a rule does not provide a local level of administration, some local administrative duties have been transferred from the State administration to municipal authorities (including land-use planning, construction, health, and some environmental matters). In these cases the appointed municipal authorities are not acting within the interest of the municipality concerned but as administrative executors of legislative rules. The decision-making of those municipal bodies is subject to appeal in regional administrative courts, not to the municipal council. In other municipal matters, which are usually based in municipal self-government, only the legality of procedures is controlled by State administrative courts. Therefore, if mere political choices of the decisions (economy, social institutions, planning, etc.) of the municipality are at stake, the decisions cannot be altered by State authorities or courts.

24. The Administration Act reflects the modern principles of openness and protection of rights. Legal standing is the basic and natural condition for acting in procedures. This concept covers all interested parties in the affected sphere of decision-making. In environmental and land-use planning, associations also have legal standing because access to justice is granted to a broader audience rather than just the parties that are directly involved in the matter (Aarhus Convention[3]). According to municipal law, every citizen in the municipality, including a registered association, is entitled to appeal against municipal decisions.

---

3. Convention on Access to Information, Public Participation in Decision-Making and Access to Justice in Environmental Matters (1998).

Chapter 3. Introduction to the Law of Property and Trust

§1. Historical Origin and Evolution

25. What is property law? Property law deals with property rights. In terms of legal disciplines, its main parts are real law or law of objects (effects, articles) and the law of obligations or contracts. There are numerous categories of property rights in the legal system regarding immovable and movable property. The main part of property law deals with the concept of ownership and the competences of owners to convey, mortgage, and lease property. In addition to this 'general' part of law, specific sectors deal with property law as well, especially heritage law, marriage law, and company law. There are also differentiations within the categories of property, both immovable and movable. In the background, general contract law may be of significant importance, especially when equity is at stake. The effect of this is that there is no need to maintain or to stress the distinction, within civil law, between contractual law and property law in the narrow sense (law of objects or things, real law). In the Finnish doctrine, property law is defined partly as the powers or subjective rights *extra partes*, partly as the law on succession of rights.[4]

26. Property law also has connections to tax law (real estate taxes), agricultural law (succession rights, farm-related subsidies), planning law (plans indicating building lots in addition to municipal development fees), and survey or formation of real estate, plus expropriation law, laws on roads and mining, nature conservation law, and more. These related areas will not be dealt with in full in this monograph.

27. Law of property has its origins in the concept of possession (Swedish '*hävd*', Finnish '*hallinta*'). Before the enactment of the Swedish General Code (1734), elements of Germanic (*Gewere*) and Roman conceptualization of possession (*proprietas*, *dominium*) were used to describe the real basis of land possession. The Code took the position in favour of traditional, mostly Germanic, concepts, which led to a less formal and open understanding of the owner or possessor and his legal position than in the case of Roman law and its later European successors. In modern times, Finnish jurisdiction emphasizes the real connection between possession and property rights. However, possession is defined as one element of ownership only, and, therefore, it has to be separated from the concept of ownership. For the transfer of ownership and the exercise of the owner's powers, other elements are relevant as well (e.g., the requirement of a formal deed and registration). Transfer of property rights is understood as a dynamic procedure which proceeds step by step to its fulfilment, not just as the result of one explicit declaration or deed. A sale may for instance be concluded as a condition of dissolution.

4. Kartio, *Esineoikeuden perusteet*, 3.

§2. The Concept of Ownership

I. Unity and Fragmentation

A. *General*

28. Ownership or property has three elements: first, the possession including powers of use; second, the categories of competence of the owner, i.e., the content of property rights (power to lease, mortgage, etc.); and third, the protection of the (right) owner in case of succession or conflict of claims from third parties. The first two elements are regulated mostly on the basis of constitutional law, and they are independent of the person of the owner (constitutional property protection).[5] The third aspect comprises rules for the examination of the 'better' or preferential right in a situation where two or more persons are claiming to be considered as owners. Decisions concerning conveyance of property rights are decisive for different legal situations concerning property rights as well, for instance, execution, taxation, mortgage, and more. In addition, limited rights to immovable property may follow analogous rules of competence (e.g., a tenant's right to mortgage his building right).

B. *Categories of Acquisition*

29. Acquisition of the title of ownership is theoretically classified into three categories. The most important and common category consists of derivative acquisition. This implies that the object previously had a legal owner from whom the buyer or other receiver derives his right. Sale of immovable property is a typical example since the authority has to ensure that the seller had a legal title to the sold property and also the right to dispose of it. The second category is original acquisition. Here the object did not have a previous owner or possessor (unclaimed property). Original acquisition is not possible for immovable property. A typical example is occupancy of abandoned movable property (dereliction). It is also, according to Finnish customary law, a common right to pick berries and mushrooms on land owned by others. This right is attached to free access to natural land and water (*usus publicus*). The collected resources become property of the picker. The same is true for cut or broken wood as far it is not intentionally left by the owner for further use.

30. The third category is extinctive acquisition. In this case the title of the previous owner ceases to exist, and a new title is created for the receiver of the property. This mode of acquisition is available for both immovable and movable property. Typical situations are expropriation (compulsory taking) and compulsory auction or executive sale of either movable or immovable property. Extinction of the predecessor's right requires specific legal mandate since the constitutional property right might otherwise be encroached. Taking possession of lost movable property is based on extinctive rather than original acquisition because the owner did not

5. Constitution 2000, s. 15.

intend to abandon his title. Abandoned movable property often falls under the rules of waste law. According to waste law, the owner usually remains liable for damage which the abandoned property may cause, and, therefore, he is at least theoretically still owner after the dereliction until someone else appropriates the object.

31. What is said here about ownership and property rights, also applies mostly to limited rights invested in the property in question (lease, usufruct, pledge).

II. Immovable and Real Property

A. General Features

32. Property rights are classified as ownership and limited rights, both in relation to immovable and movable property. Land property is based on private ownership, protected and guaranteed by the Constitution (2000).[6] Ownership is defined as an unlimited or sovereign right. This definition implies that all other rights are derived from ownership, constituting limited or specified competences. This constitutional protection means primarily that whenever compulsory measures, such as expropriation, will be taken, special legislative requirements have to be considered by the legislator. Ownership as a sovereign right does not imply that the legal order could not set limits to owners' competences. Constitutional limits of property rights are defined by the concept of 'social commitment'; this means that the use of property is subject to restrictions based on law whenever public health, State security, and similar important public interests so require (passive content). On the other hand, property right holders are not obliged to take steps in order to favour public interests (active content); passive consideration and the respect of the public's vital needs, mostly defined by law, are the formal expectation.

33. The concept of 'property' may be determined both in relation to objects (*res*) and to rights in relation to objects. Hence, the term 'property', depending on the regulatory system, may refer to both rights (ownership) and objects (real estate, buildings). The academic approach, however, is to give priority to the rights-related concept. One particular real estate may therefore be the object of different categories of property rights, of which ownership is dominant. Conveyance of real property and other property rights is regulated by the Real Estate Code (540/1995). Ownership as well as other limited rights may be acquired by the compulsory act of expropriation if there is a public need for the establishment of such a right, especially in case of zoning and planning for traffic. Also movable property (tangible objects) may be subject to different categories of rights, especially ownership and security rights.

34. Property is classified as immovable or movable in terms of objects which may be subject to personal rights. Thus, property is legally understood as rights to

6. The Constitution replaced the previous constitutional act (so-called Form of Government 1919) which included the same provision (s. 6).

objects rather than as the objects themselves because legal implications cannot be bound directly to objects. The main category of property rights is ownership. Owners have a direct and unconditional right to dispose of the property and all its parts, movable or immovable. Rights of third parties (creditors, tenants) may influence the freedom to dispose. In family and hereditary law, there are rules on joint acting in matters concerning real property. There are also other situations of joint ownership or joint limited rights. Limitations of competence may arise from public law, especially concerning the right to construct buildings or to extract resources.

B. Private and Public Property

35. In literature, a distinction has been made between private and public objects (*res privatae* and *res publicae*). As will be described later, this distinction has in practice little importance for conveyance and registration of property. The term 'public object' is used for property items which serve a public use and are mainly owned by institutions of public law, although sometimes they are owned by companies based on civil commercial law. The origin of the distinction was that property that was used for public needs was separated from that in private possession. Subsequently, the public needs were corporatized, and the public property was taken over by the Church, the State and the municipalities.[7] What is still relevant for this sector is that some parts of the property belonging to these public law institutions cannot be freely disposed of or sold (*res extra commercium*). There are still some limits on the conveyance of immovable property or property under a will. In a broader sense, public property would include land and water areas which are open to public access but which are altogether under private ownership (waterways, terrain routes).

36. A distinction has to be made between public objects and public property (*res communes omnium*) which describes a situation where the (usually immovable) property is not owned by anybody. One example in international law is the open sea; another is the atmosphere or the air. In Finnish law, this concept has lost its importance. Previously there were water and forest areas where the owners were not determined, and, therefore, these areas were open for everybody. In the nineteenth century it was still possible for a pioneer settler to occupy forest areas (appointed by the State) and to receive a title of ownership on the basis of occupancy. Nowadays this is not possible because all inhabited forests and waters beyond the limits of registered habitation areas are distributed to specific owners, in most cases to the State. The State is also the formal owner of the Finnish territorial waters and the open middle parts of large lakes. These waters are called public water areas (Act 204/1966). In the forest sector, the northern part of inhabited Finland in Lapland has been transformed into a 'Desert Area' which is mostly owned by the State (Act 62/1991). All national parks and natural parks are also property of the State (Nature Conservation Act 1096/1996).

7. These are constitutionally guaranteed autonomous corporations. In addition to this group belongs the autonomous province administration of the Åland Islands.

37. On the whole, real property (real estate) implies the existence of a right to erect buildings for housing or other purposes unless there are restrictions of use (planning and site protection). In zoning areas land-use plans determine the permitted extent and structure of constructions (Planning and Building Act 132/1999). Elsewhere, especially along the shoreline of the sea and the lakes, construction is prohibited unless there is a detailed land-use plan or a specific consent.

C. *Other Classifications of Objects*

1. Composition

38. The main classification into immovable and movable property (objects) has been explained above. Other criteria for classification may be of importance, especially when selling or mortgaging property. When identifying an object, it may be useful to determine whether it is undivided or composed of independent parts (e.g., library or furniture). An object may also have been transformed (e.g., metal into art) or mixed in a way that it loses its original composition (recycling waste to raw material). For these reasons, terms such as simple (e.g., tools, paintings), composed objects (e.g., machines), and object compositions (e.g., stores) are used to describe how they are treated in legal terms. One can assume that the object is undivided if its original parts belong to the same owner.

39. Objects are classified into divided and undivided objects depending on the result of an eventual division. If the division would cause loss of either the physical structure or the main value of the property item, it is treated as indivisible. A vessel which, as such, could be divided into parts is indivisible if it would lose its essential characteristics. From a legal point of view, this classification is relevant in the case of joint ownership of an object. If the object is divisible, each of the owners might, if it were distributed, receive a share of it. If this were not the case, joint ownership would continue, or the property would be sold and the proceeds distributed.

a. Composition of Immovable Property

40. Immovable property consists of rights to registered units of land and waters as well as all rights connected to the possession of those units (easements, buildings, integral resources). Immovable property is a term used in different legal contexts, especially the law on conveyance, heritage, taxation, expropriation and execution. The extent of the concept – what it includes – may slightly vary depending on the statutory situation. The rights to immovable property and its constituents imply that they are binding in relation to third parties, not only between contracting parties. Hence, rights based on agreements and consents between owners concerning properties may not be part of the property, for instance, in cases of conveyance unless these agreements or consents have been properly registered as part of the property in question.

41. If the owner of a registered land unit sells a defined part (parcel) of the real estate, this agreement is basically a simple transaction between the seller and buyer until the parcel sold has been legally separated and transformed into an independent unit of land and transferred to the buyer, i.e., with full ownership. In practice, however, possession may be given to the buyer in terms of the agreement in cases where the legal separation of the land has not yet been carried out. For this reason, the law (Real Estate Code, REC Chapter 10) today, as an exception, gives formal protection to the buyer of land through registration of the agreement and the defined parcel of real estate even before the legal separation of that land by a required survey measure. This means that a successor on the seller's side is bound to transfer ownership of the parcel and cannot prevent the buyer from enacting separation of the parcel to an independent unit. This category of land possession is a common way of holding a title of land ownership (which also may cover water areas).

42. A further category of immovable property is the 'right to a conditional building lot'. Historically, municipalities could not transfer ownership of land which they had received from the Crown by donation (donation land). There was a need, however, especially in the nineteenth century, to appoint areas for industries, railways, and other industrialized activities. Donation land was therefore given to operators or companies by the municipalities as conditional building lots. The donation deed gave the party permanent and full possession of the land but not full ownership which otherwise could have been transferred. One main condition was that the area was to be permanently used for its original purpose and could therefore not be altered, at least not from the original proposal. Nowadays the Real Estate Code does not recognize this category of rights; instead existing rights are treated as full ownership. This means that the owner of such a right may apply for registration of the right as a title of ownership.[8]

43. Possession of land and other real property may have its basis in contracts of lease or authoritative decisions on usufruct. In addition to lease of land or water areas, there are also limited rights to use resources of a real estate that may be based on contract and registered to be binding for later owner or tenants of the property. In principle, freedom of contract rules the content of arrangements. But not every contractual right is suitable for registration, especially not personal rights or easements. Moreover, plan provisions and survey measures may lead to the creation of limited rights, usually easements which can be replaced by contract between the parties, for instance the right to place pipelines or other installations on an estate.

8. The Supreme Court has declared that the right will not turn into full ownership if the original activity stops but the land returns to be property of the municipality (KKO 2005:42/29.3.2005). In the case, a dockyard in the centre of Helsinki closed and the detailed plan appointed the area for housing and trade purposes, which added considerably to the value of the land. The successors of the dockyard claimed, mainly on the basis of the new rules in the Real Estate Code which equalized the conditioned right with ownership, that the property should be registered under the title of ownership on its behalf in the property registry. The municipality's position was that the property was still under the previous rules of conditioned right. The court decided the matter in favour of the city.

b. Registration of Property Information

44. Today, the Real Estate Code (REC Chapter 10) has introduced explicit rules for the determination of ownership or legitimacy to real property. The real property register includes information on ownership, mortgages and other limited rights. Limited rights which encumber a property owned by another person must be registered as a special right. This applies to contractual rights (usufruct, excavation rights) which are connected to specified users. Easements between properties, if established in an administrative procedure, are automatically registered by the authority in the cadastre (land register), not in the property register.

45. Chattels and buildings may also be registered if there is a need to identify them as belonging to an industry or trade. This could be the case, for instance, if there is an economic purpose in affixing property items to activities in agriculture, manufacture and storage. Within the framework of mortgaging movable property, the chattels of a firm or company may be registered as an object for mortgage (company mortgage, see paragraph 303).

The State takes responsibility for incorrect registration based on fault on the part of the administration but not for the incorrectness of registered data concerning the deed. Registration of property rights under Finnish law is a rather recent institution. Therefore, registration is not always conclusive proof of the owner or rightholder although the register is based on the assumption of *publica fides*. The aim of the registry system is that purchasers can rely on the correctness of registered information on owners and other property rights (assumption of public reliability). The challenging of titles follows certain rules (see paragraph 419).

46. In addition to the property register on owners of real estate, there is another register (cadastre) on the physical content of individual properties (land register). This register has a long tradition, dating already from the land tax system under Swedish rule. The Finnish real estate system is comprehensively based on registration, i.e., both registers cover all property units (real estate, State land, and more). In addition, other (independent) units, mostly related to easement or servitudes, are registered in the land register, e.g., roads and so-called undivided water areas which belong by shares jointly to several parcels of real estate. The property register and the land register, which are still separately maintained, are today combined by a data-based information system (real estate information data register), which is operated by the national land survey administration. There are also other registers that are relevant for property information (farm register, private road register).

47. The information held within the land register is collected on the basis of land survey decisions. Land survey procedures function in a manner similar to jurisdiction. The decisions on survey issues concerning the formation of real estate and other units, on easements, and on restructuring of real estate for larger management projects, are official, final, and binding, both *inter partes* and *extra partes*, and cannot be contested later on in court. Publicity for the measures taken is attained partly in the procedure itself with its administrative rules of processing and partly in the registration which gives the administrative decision *publica fides* concerning real estate.

III. Movable and Personal Property

A. Conceptualization

48. The law on movable property has its roots in the commercial tradition of the Swedish General Law 1734, especially in its Commercial Code. Contract law, trade law, company law, law on immaterial rights and other jurisdictions later developed into legal fields of their own, but the rights under these regulatory orders affect property law as well. However, property rights have similar features concerning both movable and immovable property as regards contractual transfer, possession, mortgage and contracts on usufruct. From the viewpoint of property law, the law of obligations offers some legal elements which affect the validity and consequences of contractual arrangements, especially the Act on Contracts and the Promissory Notes or Bonds Act.

49. Movable property is defined negatively: movable property covers all property items which are not immovable. Property consists of rights and objects. Property rights to land other than ownership are considered movable property, for example tenancy and security rights. Physical parts of land (buildings, felled trees, etc.), if transferred to others by contract or easement, are movable objects. A building that is erected by a tenant is a movable object of real estate. After the tenancy has expired, it normally falls under specific rules to become part of the immovable property (i.e., the real estate). Rights or shares in a company or a heritage are considered to be movable property; the same is true where jointly owned property consists of immovable property, for instance, real estate. The difference between movable and immovable property becomes more evident in cases of sale or donation. In these cases, a specified form of contract and registration of conveyance is required for immovable property only.[9]

50. Movable property consists of rights that cover all kinds of movable objects, including commercial goods, commercial shares and papers, vehicles, industrial installations, and more. Property items may be physical or tangible and possessed in the proper sense. But property rights bound to bonds, obligations, and other intangibles may also have a distant relation to the basic document and such rights are – in the sense of possession or mobility – rather abstract. The title of ownership is in some cases based on registers but generally the possession of a movable object gives the assumption of ownership. Trade with movable property is regulated by internationally accepted rules and practices (Commercial Code or Trade Act 355/1987), based on the Vienna Convention 1980.[10]

---

9. Some movable objects are registrable under specific rules (vehicles, vessels, and aircrafts).
10. United Nations Convention on Contracts for the International Sale of Goods.

B. Bond Securities

51. Special, explicit legal rules apply to certain categories of movable property. In the law of obligations and contracts, bonds and debts are regulated in order to govern the relationship between the debtor and the creditor as well as their successors. In property law, those bonds may provide security which is usually a registration as mortgage. These bond securities as movable property are regulated in regard to conveyance and other transactions. Mortgaged securities may usually move freely, and a holder of security has the right to enforce his claim against the debtor or his mortgaged property.

52. Registered movable objects are generally movable property that is the supposed property of the possessor. Under contractual law, this legal assumption may be complemented by either *traditio longa manu* (a third party has possession based on notification) or *traditio brevi manu* (the possessor becomes the owner). Registration of movable property as such is therefore not required to prove ownership. Other reasons exist, requiring registration, especially traffic safety and taxation in cases of cars, airplanes, vessels, etc. Conveyance of vehicles is, as a rule, free under general contractual rules. Accordingly, the registration authority does not normally interfere with the property rights. In respect of vehicles used for public transportation, additional rules and restrictions may apply (e.g., the requirement of solvency). Since registration creates the assumption of ownership, possession, for instance, of a car is not relevant in case of a sale or a rental. Legal transactions against a debtor may include registered movables as well. In that case, the register will record the measure in order to give it validity.

C. Buildings on Other's Property

53. Buildings may legally have different status depending on the contractual or administrative situation. If nothing divergent has been agreed, buildings are part of the land property and hence in the possession of the landowner. The same is true in the case of constructions in water areas (power mills, dams, and docks). There are some important exceptions to the rule. First, in cases of land tenancy, the tenant has the right to apply for building permits and to erect buildings as an owner of the buildings. When the tenancy expires, special rules determine how the property right to the buildings are to be settled. The right may also be determined in the lease agreement. Second, in some rarer cases, land may be possessed on the basis of a so-called permanent possession (industrial lots, railway areas). If so, the erected buildings are the property of the possessor as long as the area is used for its original purpose and are at his disposal when the activity eventually comes to an end. Third, for the management of particular housing areas or local traffic, service and similar buildings for common use may be erected on the basis of easement on land and water areas. The location of the buildings requires the consent of the landowner or the decision of the survey or planning authority.

54. Immaterial rights constitute a group of movable property. The legislation follows the categories of immaterial rights, but the Act on Patents (550/1967) works as a set of general rules and principles for other immaterial rights as well. Some categories of immaterial rights have a specific connection to immovable property, especially agricultural activities such as plant breeding rights and biotechnological patents. The law on immaterial rights follows more or less the general development in the European Union and the international conventions on immaterial rights (World Intellectual Property Organization (WIPO)). The transfer and legal protection of immaterial rights is related to public interests and, therefore, some features concerning registration, licensing, etc. have been added to the law on movable property.

There are also internationally created specific categories of values or 'rights', for instance in the framework of mitigating climate change. Emission trading allowances represent a transferable property value, created in order to enforce the objectives of the United Nations Climate Change Convention (UNFCCC).[11] There are some varieties in this field. Finland participates in the EU emission trading system. Allowances are transferable between companies and other actors.

IV. Classification of Property Rights

A. *Categories*

55. According to the common understanding of property law, rights to both immovable and movable property can be classified as follows:[12]

I. Ownership of immovable or movable objects
II. Limited rights to immovable or movable property owned by others:
  1. Usufruct, rights of severance or extraction, redemption rights
    1.1. Rights presupposing possession
      – rent or leasing
      – gratuitous usufruct
    1.2. Other rights of use
    1.3. Rights of severance and extraction
      – rights to excavate land resources
      – timber-felling rights
      – rights to separate parts from an object (building, machine, equipment)
    1.4. Right to redeem objects (land, building, etc.) or part of it
  2. Value rights
    2.1. Real security rights
      – pledge, security

11. United Nations Framework Convention on Climate Change 1992.
12. Kartio, 10 et seq.

- retention of possession
- retention of ownership
- financial leasing
- assignment by way of security

2.2. Land charge (private)

- retired farmer's portion

B. Remarks on the Classification

56. The concept of usufruct and other rights to use land are understood as rights in rem, not in personam. This means that if a right has been granted by contract to a person for his own purposes, this is not a situation covered by the concept of property law. However, sometimes it may be difficult to draw a clear line. Personal rights do not remain in force after the conveyance of property. There are different ways of making contractual rights binding even in the case of transfer of ownership. Easements and leases are regulated by law, and they are valid even in cases of transfer. The same is true when the right is based on a will. In the event of expropriation of ownership of real estate, limited rights are usually not maintained, but the entitled parties receive compensation for the value of the right.

57. Separation or extraction rights are usually applicable in economic activities based on raw material. This can be any form of natural resource or construction. The taking or acquisition of minerals, however, is not possible on a contractual basis – this because the mining legislation regulates who may acquire the right to use minerals. If the minerals are located, as they frequently are, on property owned by someone else, the mining concession includes the necessary rights of extraction and entry. Additional rights may be agreed between the landowner and the holder of the mining right (Mining Act 621/2011). Moreover, one must bear in mind that the extraction and separation may – in addition to the contract – require a permit from the competent authority, particularly in cases of the excavation of soil materials, and especially with gravel and rock. Such a permit is always required when the excavated material is intended to be used other than on the real estate itself (Soil Excavation Act 555/1981). A contract cannot replace a permit which has been rejected.

58. Felling of timber is a common topic between the landowner and the buyer of wood. A timber-felling right has specific features. It is also worth noting here that the forestry legislation may restrict a contractually planned operation. In all cases, clear cutting presupposes a forest management plan which must, *inter alia*, fulfil the requirements of sustainable use of the forest land. Moreover, certain forest habitats must be observed.[13] The contract may therefore authorize the applicant for the felling right, instead of the owner of forest land, to fulfil the obligations of the Forestry

13. Habitat Directive 92/43/EEC.

Act (1093/1996). After having presented the appropriate plan to the forest authority, the cutting may start. In case of negligence, however, the authority may interrupt the measure later on.

59. Originally, a contract to buy a 'parcel' of real estate was perceived as a case of severance or extraction where the landowner remained in possession as the owner of the parcel until it was separated from the real estate. Nowadays this situation is considered to be an immediate transfer of ownership where the seller loses his competence to exercise ownership over the parcel even before it has been properly created as an independent unit in the property registry (see paragraph 84).

60. Security rights are classified as based on either their ownership or encumbrance. In instances of ownership-based security rights, the security holder (creditor) remains the owner of the object (retention of ownership). In addition, leasing belongs to this category. In the case of an encumbrance-based security right, the debtor remains as the owner (pledge, retention of possession). A retired farmer's portion is based on a contract and gives the beneficiary an ongoing right of value, usually a right to use land or a building that can be utilized for living quarters.

C. Categories of Ownership and Joint Ownership

61. In respect to immovable property, ownership of land is defined as absolute and undiversified. There is only one concept of ownership (*dominium*). The historical permanent possession of land has, in most cases, been transferred to the category of (full) ownership according to the present legislation of 1995. This means that the possessor can apply for registration of his right as owner. The title (*titulus*) gives the legal (registered) owner direct power to decide on the transfer of ownership, use it as security, and dispose of the utilization of land (real estate) as well as its resources, including the establishment of its constructions. Limited rights of use may be established by a contract. The status of ownership is the same whether the title belongs to a physical person, a corporate body, or a public corporation (State, municipality, State churches). State property can be transferred to private persons or companies, but there are some restrictions on real estate used for public or administrative purposes (public property). Similar rules apply to municipal and ecclesiastical real property.

62. Possession of movable property indicates, with some exceptions, that the holder of the object is also the owner. Possession is not a sufficient criterion in cases such as vehicles, bonds, shares, immaterial rights, and property items in general, unless the legal ground for ownership is in the object itself. However, this is not the case if ownership needs registration or reference to a share register.

1. Joint Ownership

63. In cases of joint ownership, the owners act jointly together, which means that one of the owners cannot dispose of the object or a part of it alone. Joint ownership – as well as joint possession of the object – is classified as either real (fractional) co-ownership or indivisible joint ownership. The previous category is more common and regular as it occurs in cases of joint ownership of real estate or inherited property items. Each owner of a share is equally entitled to the object per capita. Both immovable and movable objects may be jointly owned (Act on Joint Ownership 180/1958). Also the right to lease property and to erect constructions is subject to joint possession. Property under joint ownership may be partitioned according to specific rules, usually by selling the property. An individual share may also be conveyed to someone else without the consent of the co-owners; one of the shareholders may buy the other shares and thus dissolve the joint situation.

64. Indivisible joint ownership occurs in situations where the property consists of an estate with undefined objects and where the property legally constitutes separate property from that of the owners. This is the case when spouses acquire property in common or when heirs have shares in an estate. For instance, real estate in a deceased estate is not jointly owned by the heirs; instead they have shares in the property as a whole (undivided estate). The heirs may only conclude transactions concerning items in the estate by acting together. In similar cases, the joint owners create an administration where, for instance, the board or a managing director has the power to act in the name of the owners. A national peculiarity of joint ownership is a share in a jointly owned area. Here, real estate parcels have for historical reasons acquired shares in adjacent joint waters or forests. These areas are not parcels themselves but rather accessory rights to the owner-real estate. The shares vary in size depending on the 'weight' of each owner-real estate as shareholder. These areas are jointly managed according to specific legislation (Act on Commons or Joint Areas 758/1989). The owners of the real estate may dispose of their shares, which may then be allocated to other real estate in a specific procedure under the law on survey.

65. There are also situations where there is one owner (or a group of joint owners) but another person (or group) must consent to the actions of the owner. In matrimony, the rule is that each spouse remains owner of the property acquired before the marriage (Marriage Act 234/1929 section 35). He or she may later also acquire property jointly as usual. During the marriage, each spouse requires the other's consent before selling property which belongs to the common household. This is also true for one's private property. In addition, the spouses have a marital right to each other's property, unless this has been excluded by contract or legacy. This is not a property right, and the spouse cannot be registered as co-owner of the immovable property. It can be viewed as a form of expectancy. After the dissolution of the marriage by divorce or death, the effect of this right is that each of the parties will receive half of the other spouse's property. In the case of death, this right goes to the heirs. In order to prevent abuse of the spouse whose property is subject to this right, there exists during the marriage certain anticipatory means to prevent the property from being essentially destroyed or its value diminished.

§3. Estate and Patrimony

I. Unity and Fragmentation

66. As a rule, property is connected to a person's will, either physical or corporate. However, in certain cases, the property as patrimony may represent a legal entity which may not be ruled by individuals. Instead it is managed by trustees, fiduciaries, or corporate representatives (estate, fund, bankrupt's estate). The legal principles for the management of estate property are similar but regulated by different laws. In civil law, the legislative structure concerning estates and patrimonies has its roots in the law on heritage (Heritage Code 40/1965). This code regulates the order of transactions in cases of statutory succession and testamentary succession. It also gives the basic definitions for estates and patrimonies as well as the administration of that kind of property. There are, however, additional rulings on undistributed property, for instance, in the Marriage Act and in the legislation on bankruptcy, taxation, and execution.

67. The Heritage Code provides rules for the interim administration of the estate and the distribution of inheritance. The inheritance right consists of three categories: the direct heirs who are entitled to legitim, i.e., a lawful portion of the heritage; other entitled inheritors; and the spouse. Direct heirs are children, adopted children, and their descendants. They are entitled to the heritage, unless there are testamentary dispositions or the surviving spouse's rights which interfere. The legitim is, basically, half of the heritage to which the direct heirs are entitled. This part cannot be set aside by testamentary disposition. Other entitled inheritors are, when there are no direct heirs, parents and subsequently, brothers and sisters of the decedent. After them, the chain continues to the grandparents and secondarily to their children. Cousins do not inherit.

68. Testamentary dispositions may be universal legacies or limited bequests. In the former situation, the beneficiary has the same status as heirs. In latter situations, the legacy will be given to the beneficiary before the estate is distributed among the entitled inheritors. A will may transfer full or limited ownership or limited rights to a property. Depending on the will, the beneficiary may thus be or not be entitled to transfer the property to others, including according to his own desire.

69. In order to be valid, the will has to be written in a legally prescribed mode. However, the involvement of a lawyer or a *notarius publicus* is not required. A will has to be in writing, with persons acting as witnesses when the will is signed. The witnesses then have to verify by their signature that the testator had signed the document which was declared to be a will; however, the witnesses do not have to know the content of the will. In cases of involuntary reason, for instance, an accident or sudden illness, a will may be pronounced orally in the presence of two witnesses, or in writing, without witnesses, by a will which is written and signed by hand. These forms of will are valid only for a maximum of three months. In order to validate the will after the death of the testator, the testament has to be officially notified to the inheritors.

II. Trust and Fiduciary Mechanisms

70. Trust does not exist within institutions in the same sense as it exists in Common Law. In Finnish civil law, trust is limited to express the institution of a fund or foundation, which, as a juristic independent person, is usually based on a testamentary disposition. Third parties (trustees or beneficiaries) do not have co-ownership in the property of a trust. The trust, therefore, has no role to play if there is a dispute on property rights invested in the foundation or company. An administrator of property belonging to a heritage or a bankrupt's estate has a limited power to dispose of the property as long as it has not been partitioned or assigned to its final owner. These competences cover only disposals which are needed for the maintenance of the property. This power may in some cases of urgency involve the sale of property on behalf of the formal owner. Similarly, it is true with regard to legal guardians of minors.

71. In competition law, trust has the international meaning of a coalition of big companies, aiming at the domination of the market. For this field of legislation, which will not be analysed here, the international trade activities World Trade Organization (WTO) and European competition law are decisive.

A. Fiduciaries

72. There are different categories of fiduciaries. Authority, written or oral, is required both for legal acts between private persons and in business activities. In these cases, authority is mostly based on agreement between the assignor and the assignee. Authority in commercial law may also follow the position which a person is given in a company. This is the case of authorization on the basis of one's position (e.g., managing director). A similar position arises when a person is empowered with general authority (procuration). In cases of empowerment, the assignee acts exclusively in the name of the assignor. He also has no right to transfer property to himself or manage property of the assignor in his own name.

B. Guardianship

73. Persons under guardianship have a guardian, either statutory or appointed (Act on Guardianship 442/1999). A statutory guardian is prescribed in circumstances where there is public interest to protect the rights of the ward or to notify the guardianship publicly. The main situation of statutory guardianship is minority.

There are also situations where the legal capacity of a person is restricted, especially in the case of bankruptcy. Appointment of guardianship requires a decision of the court and that decision may be permanent or limited to a fixed term. The guardian has to keep accounts separate from his own and to report the keeping of the accounts to the municipal board on guardianship. For legal transactions concerning the property under guardianship, the guardian needs the consent of either the court or the municipal board, depending on the importance of the transaction. Furthermore, the sale of real property requires the consent of the court. For parents, the board may grant some concessions from the need for a permit.

74. The alternative to a court declaration on guardianship is the appointment of a trustee to manage the property of a person or to act in a legal matter. This appointment is decided by the court, on the request of the person himself, relatives, or the municipal board for guardianship. The task is limited to specified legal actions.

§4. Possession and Title

75. Possession is a central concept in property law. Possession represents, in fact, the value of the property in the sense of utilization and exchange. Therefore, the legal system protects possession in different ways and also, if necessary, provides remedies for returning possession to the entitled subject. Possession is characterized as the factual situation of ownership or other right (assumption of property). However, in legal terms, possession behaves differently in the case of immovable and movable property. Possession of land or buildings does not prove ownership of the possessor, but possession of movable property, with some exceptions, implies that the possessor is the owner (*traditio*).

76. Possession of land may have its basis in the title of ownership or in other grounds for possession. In the instance of transfer of ownership, the contract usually appoints the time for the change of possession. If there is no agreement at this point, the possession passes when the contract is final and properly signed. If the transfer is connected to administrative procedures (compulsory expropriation) or court decisions (distribution of estate), possession usually passes when the decisions are final.

77. Other legal sources for possession are limited rights to a property, mainly tenancy of land or buildings, and limited rights to use natural resources (forest, gravel). There is also a variety of contractual situations with the contract usually determining the duration of possession of the rightholder. Additionally there are, in tenancy law, provisions regarding the right of the landlord to take possession of the property under tenancy. If the buildings have been erected by the tenant, there are specific rules on the settlement of the ownership and possession of the buildings. The legislation on private roads and easements provides for rules on taking possession of land belonging to other real estate parcels. These titles of possession are usually permanent, and they may also imply a right to erect necessary buildings and other constructions. The titles are also protected by registration in the land register.

78. An immemorial possession is a historical relic which holds relevance today. The concept describes situations where the possession of a person started long before anyone could remember how possession was originally obtained.[14] The provision usually covers limited areas for fisheries or sites for construction, but it applies also to real estate. As a title of ownership, immemorial possession cannot supersede boundaries which have been marked in a survey procedure. In practice, immemorial possession could hardly nowadays provide ownership to real estate. Permanent possession without ownership may still be successful in terms of limited rights of utilization.

79. Typically joint ownership leads to joint possession of a property. The decision on how to share possession requires the consent of all shareholders of the undistributed property, for example, the estate or company. The parties may enter into a contract in which they assign to each entitled shareholder an individual possession. Joint possession may be dissolved by a court decision or, in the case of land, by a survey distribution. If there is a contract, it may serve as a basis for partitioning ownership in those procedures as well.

14. The provision has its origin in the Swedish General Law 1734 (Land Code Ch. 15, s. 1), which still is valid in cases where the possession existed before the entry into force of the present Real Estate Code (1 Jan. 1997).

Part I. Immovable and Real Property

Chapter 1. General Classification

80. Property law is dominated by two aspects: civil and administrative law. Civil law rules over the competences of owners and other entitled right holders and their powers to enter contracts, to possess, and to use the property as security. Public law regulates the relationship between owners and the society, basically the competent authorities. Management of a property may require administrative decisions, planning approvals, permits, and more. Contracts within the area of public law are therefore conditioned or guided by authorities. For instance, the contents of a contract concerning building rights depend on the public admissibility of construction.

81. As a rule, land ownership is a uniform right, without regard to the legal status of the owner. Thus, it is of no significance for the content of property rights if the owner or rightholder is a private person, a company, a municipality or the State. The origin of ownership may vary, especially in the case of State-owned land which often is not based on conveyance but on historical reasons. The State, municipalities, and other public corporations may also acquire land by compulsory measures, especially expropriation. Differences in origin may appear in the land registry system.

82. Planning law influences the development of land property units. In areas with detailed plans (zoning), the units are mostly building lots and public areas; in other areas, real estate is formed by different survey procedures. In planned areas, the restrictions to build and to form or divide real estate originate from the plan itself, whereas in other areas, the restrictions are of a more general nature and are based on law. Legally and economically, the different categories of real estate do not show important diversities. All categories may, for instance, be used as security or tenancy in a comparable manner. However, some objects as public areas and land acquired by expropriation may be subject to restrictions in those respects.

83. The owner may use his property as financial security for a mortgage. Other contractual commitments may also be substantially secured by mortgage, for instance a lease of land and rights of extraction. In the case of a sale of a parcel – which is not yet a unit in the register but only a contractually defined part of a real estate – the buyer has to apply for the registration of his title in the same way as a buyer of a whole real estate. Therefore, there is no need in this event to mortgage the buyer's right to separate the sold part of the property of the seller. The same applies to a buyer of a share in a jointly owned real estate. After the registration, he has the same position in the joint relationship as the seller. After the sale, the seller of a parcel or a share may no longer use the sold property as security for his own commitments, even if the parcel has not yet been separated and registered as a unit of its own. However, a statutory lien or a lease may continue to encumber the property in the hands of the buyer. Separation of the parcel or the share from its previous position as part of real estate and the creation a unit in the real estate registry require formation (demarcation) in land survey.

Chapter 2. Legal Interests

§1. Land Register System

I. Property Registration

84. Real property is registered in two registers. The land register (cadastre[15]) identifies existing real estates as physical units. It also gives information about easements and land which belong in common to certain real estate (common land). The other register, the property rights register or property register, indicates the legal rights concerning the units.

85. The property or title register[16] gives information about ownership, securities and further conditions concerning the title. Both acquisition of the title and the existence of special or limited rights will be registered. If the owner requires security for his acquisition of title to real estate – which again requires certain sale formalities – the acquisition must be registered. Registration as such is not a legal criterion for ownership, but it is necessary for the later sale or mortgaging of the property. The provisions on the registration of title also apply to the registration of acquisition of units, which are not units in the land register, namely a share and a parcel of real estate, a common land (of real estate), a parcel, and a share of a common land.

86. This register actually has two functions – the identification of the title holder and the economically relevant measures burdening the title in case of conveyance of the title. Since only one mode of land ownership exists, the land survey register does not provide information about the land being privately or publicly owned. However, State land taken for specific purposes, for example, natural parks or open sea areas, are registered as specific real estate in the register. Thus, this register gives information about the history of survey measures, area, borders as well as servitudes and specific restrictions or conditions concerning land or its utilization.

87. The real property register is administrated by the Ministry of Agriculture and Forestry (Act 584/2009)). The handling of applications and the collection of information is the duty of the local register authorities. The competent authority was originally the district court where the real estate is located but today that function is given to the land survey authority. The information contained in the register is freely available to authorities, including duties concerning property rights, land survey and land-use planning.

II. Land Register (Cadastre)

88. The real estate register (land register) gives information about the geographical location and other technical specifications of real estate, as well as the physical

15. In Finnish: kiinteistörekisteri.
16. In Finnish: lainhuuto- ja kiinnitysrekisteri.

interrelation between real estate regarding the use of that real estate, especially easements.[17] The information on real estate and other registered units does not depend on the title of ownership. In the register, 'real estate' is a comprehensive concept for different categories of the same legal state, namely 'register units'. What is common to all real estate is that the term assigns independent register units with full ownership. The main categories of real estate in the broad sense are two: real estate within the narrow sense (regular land units outside zoning areas for housing and other activities, e.g., farming, forestry, and industry), and building lots in town planned (zoning) areas. Other categories of real estate are, *inter alia*, expropriation units, conservation areas, public areas (in a town planned area for public purposes), and forest areas owned by the State, as well as public roads. Water areas may also be formed as real estate, but they are mostly parcels of real estate or common areas jointly owned by several real estates; that means that commons are appurtenances of the entitled real estates. In the register, a real estate is organized according to its location (region, municipality, locality and quarter).

III. Reasons for Registration

89. Real estate (in a broader sense) is the basic registry unit and the central concept in the law in respect of land property and immovable property. In addition, limited parts of real estate, such as parcels, are within the regime of immovable property and may be used as security but are not marked in the land register. The content of land ownership covers all resources, constructions, and immovable parts of land (vegetation) on and under the surface, including water, minerals, forests, and more. The land register, therefore, also gives information about valuable resources and may serve as a data base for taxation and trade. The property register shows who eventually has a contractual or limited right to use parts of or resources on real estate, or what kinds of mortgage are valid. If a property is under lease, the construction on the leased land may belong to the leaseholder and is therefore legally movable property (see paragraph 131).

90. The main reason for registration of property rights and real estate is to maintain *publica fides* for existing property conditions and thus provide a secure basis for transactions and securities as well as for administrative decision-making. This task could not be met otherwise because the law does not recognize officials as notaries to act as providers of data on property rights and real estate. Instead, certificates and other documents on property conditions delivered by register officials and other authorities must be based on the data information contained in those two registers. In the following chapters, the property or title registration system will be described in more detail.

91. Second, the property register provides necessary information for transfer of ownership and for the establishment of limited rights as securities, mortgages, and

17. Land Register Act 392/1985.

more. The property register may also, if the competent Ministry (Agriculture) prescribes, contain personal information regarding owners and titleholders of rights in relation to the property in question.[18] The land register again provides reliable information for all kinds of transactions and administrative measures regarding objects, including the history of formation, limited rights connected to the estate (easement, restrictions of use), and the planning situation.

92. The information on registered titles and rightholders is presumed to be correct unless otherwise proved in court. In order to ensure correctness for registration, some deeds, such as conveyance of ownership to real estate must be performed in a specific procedure, confirmed by a *notarius publicus*. This is an exception from the general rule of contractual liberty. An agreement concerning conveyance without the appropriate and formal procedure is not binding against third parties, but is still valid as an agreement between the two parties. While such an agreement may not support court proceedings to enforce the intended conveyance, it may, if not respected by the parties, have contractual consequences in terms of compensatory obligations.

93. The information held within the two registers is decisive for all contexts where property details, titles, and limited rights to individual properties are dealt with (i.e., authorities, financing companies, sales managers, etc.). However, the legal position of registered, and thus assumed, ownership or other rights can be contested in court on specific grounds (see paragraph 423), but that is exceptional and occurs when the registration history is not clear. Possession and other elements relating to the succession of ownership will then be determined by the court in order to solve property disputes. But as long as this is not the case, the information of the register cannot be disregarded or contested.

94. The information concerning objects, existing real estate, their areas, borders, and other features has its origin in the land register which thus is the geographic basis for the registration system of property rights. In cases of conveyance of real estate, information on sales and other transfers of rights is provided to the property register by the authority or person acting as notary. The notification of the notary must identify personal data of the parties to the sale and provide other information as stipulated by decree of the government. The register of notaries will in turn identify the person who testified to the deed. He may eventually have to give evidence or other information in a dispute on the circumstances surrounding a deed.

IV. Formation of Real Estate and Other Units

95. The land register also includes separate land units which are not independent parcels but areas or parcels with limited rights (other register units). Especially

18. This information would be transferred to the property register from the official population register. The corresponding is true for companies and other corporations for the information which is collected in a public trade register.

common are water and forest areas which belong by shares to several real estates. The shares represent accessories to real estate, similar to easements and large parts of private water and forest areas are registered as these commonly owned units. The shares are registered under each real estate as well as an appurtenance. Private roads are also registered as other units. These roads have been established as easements in accordance with the Private Roads Act (358/1962). Nowadays public roads are expropriated with full ownership and are, therefore, real estate in the category of expropriation units.[19]

96. All information concerning real estate and other registered units is collected from the survey procedures and comparable measures carried out by the survey administration.[20] The regulation concerning the formation of real estate depends on the subcategory. In principle, there are no general restrictions concerning the distribution of real estate or incorporation of parcels or real estate within each other. Formerly, the splitting of real estate was limited mainly due to tax reasons. The conditions concerning the formation of real estate in the narrow sense and building lots differ to some extent, as building lots must be produced exactly as they appear in the detailed plan and the lot distribution plan, which in turn have to follow the town plan. However, as far as civil law is concerned, conveyance, lease, and mortgage are practically the same, and there are no differences between the above two categories of real estate (in the broad sense).[21]

97. The two registers which formerly were kept by different authorities are today combined to form a comprehensive real property register, kept by one authority (regional land survey authority) but still with these two different registers within the system. For the coordination of the registers, a data-based information system is operated by the National Land Survey. This 'service', however, is kept on a technical basis and does not, as a rule, establish specific or additional liability to the managing body. Liability for errors in the registers is regulated separately for each register.

§2. Immovable Property

I. Land and Fixtures

98. Fixtures are, by definition, movable or immovable, depending on their functional and physical connection to a building or industrial equipment. As a rule, fixtures which cannot be removed without destroying their location are parts of the immovable property (e.g., heating and sanitation systems, floors, and elevators). Outdoor fixtures, such as bridges, water pumps, etc. are treated analogically. In

19. With the exception of limited rights to build a bridge over someone's property or a tunnel underneath (Public Roads Act 503/2005).
20. The Act on Formation of Real Estates (554/1995).
21. See Decision of the Supreme Court, Yearbook 2010:35: A real estate was partitioned and the building consisting vertically of two apartments was divided accordingly.

cases of compulsory measures, for example, execution, mortgaging, expropriation, and more, these rules are binding in order to protect the right holders of the real estate in question. In voluntary situations of transfer, the seller may, if technically possible, be allowed to remove fixtures of the real property. Under cultural and heritage rules, historical and cultural fixtures may be protected; in these cases, a separation of fixtures may be prohibited, or it may require the consent of the competent authority.

II. State-Owned Land and State Leases

99. As illustrated above, in general, State property legally has the same content and limits as private property. Most State-owned land and water areas are located in nature zones, especially in national parks and other preserves, forests as well as (public) waters. The areas are administrated by different ministries; however, the State may also acquire land for agricultural purposes and convey it under specific legislation to farmers. If land is leased to private persons, the general legislation on land lease applies.

100. In built-up areas the State holds real estate for both representative and administrative purposes and also for general economic purposes. The legislation on State property regulates transfer of non-economic areas and buildings to private persons and bodies, including municipalities. The State may enter into an exchange of land with local municipalities for different reasons, though mostly within planning of housing and traffic areas; and these are deeds under general law.

101. Historically, the State (Crown or Emperor) may have granted public land for various purposes, especially for the establishment or enlargement of cities or to be used by institutions (such as universities). During the seventeenth, eighteenth, and nineteenth centuries, the legislation on land property was not well developed, and subsequently, it was not always clear whether the occupier had full ownership or permanent usufruct (cf. 'fee simple') to land and buildings. The present legislation does not recognize State grants implying limited ownership. The position of the historical holders of permanent possession is today considered to include full ownership and possession, without a legal possibility for the State-donor to interfere later in that legal position.

102. Moreover, municipalities as autonomous (self-governmental) units have transferred land to especially industrial activities on the basis of fee simple (conditioned permanent possession of real property). This institution has lost its legal basis in the present legal system, and this real estate has reached the same legal status as 'fully' owned real estate. In accordance with the rejection of limited ownership in favour of full ownership, reversion to the State is not recognized as a legal possibility. The possession can be returned by a voluntary conveyance of ownership only, or under specific constitutional conditions, by a compulsory purchase (expropriation).

III. Concept, Characters and Social Function

A. Constituent Parts and Appurtenances of Property

103. The notion of an object, immovable or movable, implies that the object as a whole may be composed of legally different constituents. If an object is subject to a legal act, especially conveyance, all constituent parts are theoretically to be covered by that act. Constituent parts are, generally, not separable from the object without destruction or reduction of value. These parts belong to buildings and other immovable constructions owned by the same assignor, such as growing woods or woodlands, soil materials, and more. If resources were separated before the transaction, they usually remain with the assignor unless otherwise agreed upon. The reason for this is that the physical separation from the object means loss of the status as a constituent part. Instead, they become appurtenances which as a rule do not follow the transaction. If a sold property has been leased and the tenant has erected a building, this building is not considered to be a constituent part of the object. If the assignee would be entitled to terminate the lease agreement, the fate of that building will be settled on the basis of the Land Lease Act (258/1966): the leaseholder may move his building away or, under specific conditions, the new landowner may redeem the ownership of the building belonging to the leaseholder. Other appurtenances of real property which belong to the assignor after the transaction are, for example, movable machineries and vehicles, furniture, and stored agricultural products.

B. Identification

104. Movable objects may also imply a division of constituent parts and appurtenances. Difficulties may arise when the object is composed of separable parts which were originally intended to be kept together. This may be the case with collections or libraries. If, hence, a library is sold, books and shelves are mostly constituent parts of the object, based on the status of the collection as it was when the transaction was entered into. In some cases, however, the books might merely be appurtenances if the value and interest of the assignee was in the historical furniture. If so, the intention of the parties should then be made clear in the deed. The constituent parts of a registered vehicle are all of its technical parts but also all of its documents which relate to the identification of the vehicle.

§3. The Defence of Property

105. According to the Finnish Constitution 2000 (section 15) public measures affecting property rights can be enacted by law only if the act provides for a public need and guarantees full compensation. If these conditions are not satisfied – if, for instance, the need is of a private character (company) – the enactment requires the legislative procedure of a constitutional act. Compulsory taking (expropriation) is generally regulated by the Expropriation Act (603/1977). There are also, for historical reasons, some specific laws on expropriation. The general act applies to varying situations. If a plan requires conveyance of land to the municipality (settlement area) or to the State (national defence), the procedure runs according to the general act. The land-use plan must be approved beforehand by the planning authority, the municipal council, according to the Land Use and Building Act (LUBA 132/1999).

106. In rare cases, ratification of a plan by a state authority (regional environmental centre) is required. If a privately owned area is planned to be included in a national or natural park or another public preserve, according to the Nature Conservation Act (1096/1996), then the administrative procedure is expropriation. In standard cases, the precondition for expropriation is a taking permit issued by the State Government, e.g., in case of pipelines, energy plants, traffic areas, etc. In specified cases, especially in planning, the approved plan or administrative decision replaces the taking permit.

§4. URBAN PROPERTY

107. In Finland, there is no legally relevant distinction between urban and rural properties. Moreover, it is of no significance whether real estate is located within a town or another municipality due to the unification of municipal law. Instead, land-use planning has certain influences on the legal position of real estate. In areas where a detailed (zoning) plan has been adopted, built-up areas will be formed in accordance with the plan and imply the building right which the plan allows. Thus, the final effect of a plan is to create various building lots as real estate in a specific order (building lot). A building right on a lot provided in a plan can be subject to contractual transfer. On the other hand, in the case of an amendment to that plan, the building right may not enjoy substantial protection (compensation) if the building right diminishes or even disappears. The protection is guaranteed basically if the plan has been enforced, and the lot has been built on in accordance with that plan.

108. Historically, the State (Swedish or Russian Crown) has granted land for the creation or enlargement of cities and for other public purposes (railways, universities, etc.). Granted land is nowadays mostly treated as regular land under property, belonging to the grant-holder. Again, cities may have granted land for specific, especially industrial, purposes (permanent right of possession). In these cases, the possessor acts as the legal owner of land as long as the original activity endures. If the activity ceases, the city may use its right of recovery; however, in practice this is not always so clear. The issue may become crucial when, for instance, a former harbour area in the central part of a city would be earmarked for housing, and the market value of that area may rise considerably.

109. Finnish law recognizes only 'flat' real estate, whereas three-dimensional utilization of land does not affect the real estate structure (see discussion of sub-building, paragraph 167). If, for instance, a built-up area is located over a railway or a harbour, the mutual rights are regulated by the categories of usufruct or easement, which are often based on expropriation. As well, space underground, without natural contact to the activities above ground, may be appointed for different operations, which may set limits to the use of the real estate above. Three-dimensional land-use in cities requires a land-use plan or an expropriation permit.

§5. Agrarian Property

110. The Finnish real estate registry system does not recognize farms as entities of property; instead, they are listed in the agricultural administration for financial purposes. Previous restrictions against acquiring agricultural land were abolished when Finland joined the European Union. However, the national agricultural policy supports and steers the creation and management of agricultural and forestry land. Here the concept of a farm and viable agriculture play a role for structuring land-use and the formation of economic units (Farm Financial Aid Act 329/1999). Environmental subsidy may be used either for supporting production or for environmental protection; an example of this may be subsequent restrictions against the use of fertilizers along watercourses.

111. Farms are, in principle, owned by the farmers themselves. Additional land may be leased to improve the economy, but entire farms may also be acquired under lease. For this reason, the farm units are rather small. Company-owned large farms are not common but legally possible.

§6. Publicity of Immovable Property

I. Property Register System

112. The title or property register consists partly of a register of (property) titles, including special or limited property rights and partly of a register of mortgage for lien. The title and mortgage register is maintained for purposes of identification, publicity and legal protection (REC, Chapters 5–9). The mortgage of lien register is based on the same information and is part of the dual register system. The real estate as registered units is identified in the land register (for cadastre, see paragraph 88), which delivers the essential and reliable information to the property register. Entries regarding other rights to and encumbrances over real estate are also identified in the property (title and mortgage) register (REC Chapter 5, section 1). The regional survey authority, in whose jurisdiction the real estate is located, acts as the competent registering authority. The Act on the Title and Mortgage Register (584/2009) and related regulations contain further provisions on the establishment, opening, and keeping of the title and mortgage register.

113. An application for registration of property must inform the authority about specific details of the property (REC Chapter 6, section 1). The application must include essential information about the property, the applicant and anything else required by law. The application must be in writing and signed by the applicant or the person drawing up the application. The necessary documents must be attached to the application. The applicant may present his application orally, if the matter appears clearly from the documents and unless otherwise provided below. Conveyance is liable to taxation.[22] A registration becomes pending when the application has been presented or delivered to a competent registering authority (*lis pendens*). The application must be accepted, even if it is unaccompanied by a transfer duty receipt. An entry regarding the pending registration must be made in the title and mortgage register without delay. Information on the conveyance of real estate and other acquisitions may be entered into the title and mortgage register ex officio before an application for the registration of title is made; in certain cases, authorities may, for reasons of the clarity of the register, give information on acquisition.

114. The registering authority has a duty to provide clarification in accordance with the official principle (REC Chapter 6 section 4). Thus the authority must on its own initiative obtain the necessary information on circumstances relevant to the consideration of the matter as is available from the title and mortgage register and the other registers accessible to the registering authority.[23] If it is claimed that a right of a third party exists, which precludes the registration, and the claim is reasonably substantiated, or the right of the applicant is otherwise subject to dispute, the registering authority must call upon the person with the burden of proof to have the matter resolved in a trial within a set time limit.

115. In certain cases, registration requires the consent of a third party related to the right in question, for instance, under the law on joint ownership or marriage law. If there is a need for further investigation before a decision can be made, the application is placed in abeyance, and the applicant will be called upon to show, within a set time limit, whether a barrier to registration still exists. However, the application may not be rejected before the applicant has been afforded an opportunity to be heard.

116. A decision on registration must be made without delay and in accordance with the application, unless there is a barrier to the same. A legal circumstance that arises after the application has become pending does not preclude registration. The registration decision is performed by entering it into the title and mortgage register. The content of the decision is indicated by the registrar. If the matter is not decided in accordance with the application, the applicant will, in addition, receive a separate copy of the decision. A certificate on the register entry or a separate decision issued to the applicant is the final instrument in the matter.

22. The Transfer Duty Act (931/1996) contains provisions on the documents subject to property transfer duty which falls due at the time of application for registration.
23. A court shall notify the register authority on any pending trial concerning the cancellation or invalidity of an acquisition of real estate or a conflict of rights to the real estate, as well as on its decision and whether the decision has become final. The same applies to an action for the deletion of a register entry or its correction.

117. The property (title and mortgage) register contains the applications for registration, information on their consideration, and the decisions regarding registration. This information will be entered by the registering authority. In addition, information regarding executive measures, precautionary measures, and the bankruptcy of the titleholder of the real estate, as well as other information on rights to and encumbrances over the real estate, will be entered into the register when notified by other authorities.

118. The information in the register is subject to public access. The registering authorities issue certificates from the register upon request. The Ministry of Justice may provide access to information as a mass delivery referred to in the Personal Data File Act (523/1999).

II. Liability for Damage Caused by Technical Errors

119. A person who has suffered damage as a result of an evident misprint or miscalculation, error caused by a technical fault or another comparable error or defect in the title and mortgage register, or an instrument or certificate issued from it shall have the right to due compensation from State funds.

120. If the damage is caused by an error in the information entered into the title and mortgage register, compensation shall not be covered by the Real Estate Code. The keeper of the land register is liable for compensation only for damage caused by errors in the contents of that register, not of those in the deeds. If an authority other than the registering authority has issued an erroneous or an incomplete certificate from the title and mortgage register, and the error or incompleteness is not a result of an error in the contents of the register, the compensation will be paid from the funds of the competent public authority.

III. Correction of Errors

121. Entered registration may have errors. If a material error, i.e., one which affects the legality of the registered right, is due to false information or evidently mistaken application of the law material, the registering authority may erase its erroneous decision and decide the matter anew. Such a material error may be corrected only if all parties whose rights are affected by the correction have been heard, and all parties whose rights decrease due to the correction have consented to it. In the case of a minor or technical error, based on an evident misprint, miscalculation, or another comparable error or defect in the title and mortgage register, the registering authority may make the necessary corrections to the entries. Before the correction, those interested parties who are known to the register authority and who may suffer damage from the correction shall be afforded an opportunity to be heard. The rules for the correction procedure are similar to those applying for the registration. The correction of an error shall as soon as possible be noted on the erroneous instrument, or, alternatively, a new instrument shall be issued. An erroneous instrument or certificate shall be presented, upon request, to the registering authority for correction.

IV. Appeal

122. A final registration decision made by the registering authority shall be subject to appeal before a Court, in this case the land court. The deadline for an appeal is thirty days from the decision against which the appeal is brought. The decision of the Court of Appeal in a registration issue shall be subject to appeal before the Supreme Court if a leave to appeal is granted, as provided in Chapter 30 of the Code of Judicial Procedure (4/1734).

Chapter 3. Limited Rights

§1. Usufruct

I. General

123. Usufruct is not used as a uniform legal concept. Instead it is a loose cover for different forms of rights which are specifically regulated. The establishment of a usufruct and the most important rights of use are regulated by law. Two of the most important are land lease and house rent. A usufruct agreement may provide for the possession of the object, which is the case in lease and rent, or for the limited use of a specified object for a defined purpose. The latter cases, if not intended to fulfil the requirements of lease or rent, are quite free for contractual arrangements but, on the other hand, are not necessarily valid in the case of sale (e.g., a boat dock or a well). The beneficiary of such a contract may under certain conditions apply for the registration and obtain protection of his rights in case of transfer to third parties. If the need is permanent for a property, the need may also be established as an easement between the registered units.

124. In addition to specific rights and limitations, the legislation recognizes legal limits and conditions of use, which, since they have an overall validity, do not lead to the establishment of specific rights. This is the case when a landowner requires a permit from an authority to use his land, which permit will not be granted for reasons set by law. For example, there is a prohibition to erect a building closer than five metres to a neighbour's property without the consent of the owner of the property in question. There are also some rights to use a property directly based on law. The Finnish system recognizes that it is only possible for everyone to pass through private natural land or water if one does so without causing damage to the household or cultivated land (*usus publicus*).

II. Concept, Constitution and Statutory Provisions

125. Other situations where usufruct may occur are in sale of property, testamentary provision and transfer of rural enterprises. A contract of sale may dispose of the parties' rights to use the object or a part of it in a way that differs from the general rules on transfer of the object (see paragraph 329). Usufruct may also be created in a will: instead of ownership, a person may bequeath the right to use a property for a determined period of time (Heritage Code, Chapter 12).

126. In Finnish law, severance and redemption are usually treated separately from usufruct. The main reason for this is that the object does not remain the property of the owner after the fulfilment of the specified right. Separation of wood and gravel from the ground gives the holder of the extraction right ownership of the material. Furthermore, the release of the tenant's building by the landowner – or conversely the redemption by the tenant of a building belonging to the owner's estate – leads to a permanent change in the structure of the object.

III. Subjects and Object

127. In general, usufruct has a contractual basis; often usufruct is established in an administrative procedure by a decision of an authority. An authority may also, in relation to a permit or planning issue, ratify a contract between parties. The distinction between usufruct and easement may not be obvious in cases where an authority constitutes a right to use the property for a project, for example, utilizing water or the use of a private road. By definition, usufruct is aimed at serving a person, albeit as the owner of real estate, whereas easement creates a usually permanent relationship between two registered units.

128. The distinction between easements and other rights to use immovable property for permanent purposes is legally not important because both categories are registered as servitudes between real estate in the land register. The system of easements will be presented below (see paragraph 207).

IV. Content

129. A usufruct usually entitles the holder of the right, who is often the possessor of land or constructions, to use the property of someone else. There are no restrictions on the content of a usufruct; essentially, there are only the general principles on equity and rationality in contract law. A contract on the usage may be registered according to the provisions of the Real Estate Code, but many modes of usufruct are not registrable. In practice, also contractual usufructs are binding on the successors of the parties, at least if the assignee is able to prove the existence of such a right.

V. Extinction and Liquidation

130. Contractual arrangements are valid according to general principles of contract law. If a contract has not been in writing, and the parties have been succeeded by others, the burdened party may succeed in his claim to discontinue the usufruct, unless the entitled party provides proof of his right. Usufruct may as such be valid for an undetermined period of time. If the use is part of an activity or construction for which a permit has been granted, the usufruct lasts as long as the permit or the activity is in force. In such cases, the usufruct does not necessarily terminate without an explicit contract or prescription of the authority in question.

§2. Building and Farming Rights

I. Concept

131. Building and planting rights are included in the ownership of land. Conveyance of real estate covers all dimensions of ownership. There is, therefore, no need to create or establish building or planting rights separately. An owner may, however, dispose of the dimensions of his competence and transfer building or planting rights. These agreements are usually lease, rent or easements. If the real estate is a building lot, its value, especially in planned areas, is based on the available building right which essentially determines the value of the property. Parts of building rights are transferable as property units if the ownership of a real estate is organized as joint ownership, for instance in a company. Real estate is often owned by housing companies (*condominium*) or real estate companies. Owners of shares are entitled to the possession of an identified building or a part of it. The portion of possession depends on the share and the statutes of the company.

132. A contract of sale may provide for the creation of building rights to the acquirer of the property. A municipality or the State may sell a development area or stall land to a developing company which expects to receive building rights in the land-use plan. The assignment of building rights in the plan may be a condition for the validity of the sale. A building right for a lot may also be an object for a future sale. If, for instance, the first acquirer withdraws from the development project, he may, after the adoption of the plan, sell the lot including the not yet exercised building right. Such a sale of 'air' is legally valid, but the sale does not prevent the municipality as the planner to abolish the building assignment in a later modification of the plan. Such a loss is a risk of the developer, and, as rule, the municipality is not liable to compensate it, provided that the first contract states otherwise.

133. Similar basic rules apply to farming rights. There is no category of farming rights as a title of possession of land. Public supranational law may set limitations for planting rights of specific plants or products, and a production quota is bound to the farming unit. Farming rights belonging to the landowner may be transferred by regular contracts, especially lease and, occasionally, as a usufruct based on heritage or a will. Lease contracts of rural land have a limited duration. The holder of a planting right (farmer) may be entitled to erect buildings which are his property. The products of the land-use are also his property. In the present European context, farms receive subsidies in accordance with the Common Agricultural Policy (CAP) where the subsidy is bound to the farming units. This also means that a farmer cultivating leased farm land is entitled to the subsidy (see paragraph 158 below). In heritage law, there are specific provisions for 'keeping the farm in the family' in case the unit would otherwise be split up between numerous heirs (Heritage Code, Chapter 25). These arrangements are enforced in the context of the distribution of ownership and not by creating limited farming rights.

II. Building Rights

A. *Concept*

134. A building right has two definitions, one in relation to planning and public law, the other referring to contract or private law. Within public law, a building right constitutes the amount and purpose of buildings on a property foreseen or allowed by the planning or land-use system. Thus, for instance, a zoning plan prescribes technically how and to what degree a lot can be developed for a building. In areas where no detailed plan exists, for example, in rural areas, the assumption is that each real estate can, if geographical and environmental conditions are fulfilled, be used for building, and thus the property value includes a building option (basic building right). There are, however, several modifications to this rule of assumption.

135. In cases where this option is assumed to exist, an administrative measure, for instance, nature conservation, may lead to a compulsory measure (expropriation), and the building right may be compensated by the State or the municipality. In tax law, the rate of real estate tax depends on the existence of a building right, which may also be a non-fulfilled option. Detailed land-use planning or zoning may then, depending on the objective and content of the plan, confirm or reject the existence of building rights. Moreover, 'new' building rights may arise if, for instance, blocks for settlement or offices are foreseen in the plan. In detailed planned areas, there is also an obligation to adopt or to erect buildings in accordance with the plan. As a sanction, the municipality may later on, after demanding fulfilment of the obligation, expropriate the lot.

136. In private law, building rights, eventually separate from the real estate, appear as conveyable property. Landowners may, for instance, sell or lease the right to a developer, and that right may serve as security.[24] Nowadays, a municipality may enter an agreement with developers in order to promote construction and infrastructure of larger planning areas. The basis is that the developers are promised by the land-use plan a certain amount of new building rights, partly as a compensation for realizing the area for housing. These land-use agreements are mainly within the public law system due to the connection to the later adoption of a plan.[25] Still, the plan may set aside the conditions of the agreement, which again may have contractual consequences for the contracting municipality. In case of movable property, a habitation share company may sell the right to additional floors or another part of the building rights belonging to the property.

B. Urban Building Right

1. Concept, Constitution and Statutory Provisions

137. Building rights are based on public law, partly directly in provisions of the Constitution and legislation and partly in administrative procedure, especially ratified land-use plans and building permits. The constitutional provision on property rights protection (Constitution, section 15) implies that the value of a real estate includes the theoretical potential of building rights. Should this value be lost, for

24. See, e.g., the decision of the Supreme Court 1999:128/23.12.1999: the purchase price of land included the value of a building right in accordance with the zoning plan.
25. Decision of the Supreme Administrative Court 3124/31.10.2011: sale of land included a condition that the agreement was valid only if a future plan granted new building right to the purchaser.

instance, through a conservation measure, the value ought to be compensated.[26] The amount of an existing or a calculated building capacity depends on the planning situation. Land-use planning consists of three levels of planning. Two levels represent general planning (regional and general plans), and the lowest one, detailed planning (zoning) in a municipal area.

138. Beyond detailed planned areas, real estate is supposed to expect the construction of one building for private use. However, in coastal areas, the building requires a detailed plan; in some cases, the allowance is based on a general plan. In all cases, the creation of a building site (lot) presupposes a building permit, issued by the municipal building supervision authority. Therefore, there is no building right or building potential without such a permit. The role of land-use plans is to serve as guidance for the permit authority; they are not in themselves sufficient permission for constructing buildings. The provisions of a detailed plan are binding on the authority. Deviations from plans or constructing without a required plan may be accepted if the legal conditions for granting an exemption order exist.

2. Building Lots in Zoning Areas

139. A detailed municipal plan must set out a comprehensive and exact scheme for the modes of land-use in a limited part of a municipality (or coastal region, coastal plan). A detailed plan must be adopted when the degree of settlement and other urban activities increase.[27] The Ministry of Environment may give an order to a municipality to start planning if this obligation is not followed up otherwise.

3. Acquisition and Content

140. As described above, the content and the technical amount of individual building rights depend on the provisions of public law. Land-management contracts between the municipality and the landowner or developer may imply a certain, contractually defined building right. However, the enforcement of such contracts presupposes a planning decision as well. Therefore, contracts are conditioned by the future planning decision – which usually goes in line with the contract, since the municipality also has the planning competence. The planning procedure is subject to legal provisions on sustainable planning and participation, which may lead to some limitations or modifications of what was originally agreed upon between the parties. Such a contract, including the conditioned building right, may eventually be transferred to a third party if not forbidden by the contract.

---

26. See the decision of the Supreme Court 1997:210/31.12.1997: compensation for expropriated property should be determined according to average market price at seizure, despite a later loss of market value.
27. A detailed land-use plan must not be unreasonable for the landowner unless a public planning interest is at stake (decision of the Supreme Administrative Court 2008:14/29.2.2008). In this case usually full compensation for the loss is provided.

141. An urban building right is a concept of public law because it has its origin in the planning system (zoning). As mentioned above, the building right is one dimension of land ownership and cannot be separated to a property unit of its own. 'Land' as the object of ownership includes all constructions over and under the surface. Buildings and bridges crossing private lots are not property units but installations with a permanent right of possession. The same is true for underground constructions, tunnels, public shelters, etc. Those 'slices' of possession are usually formed through compulsory taking (expropriation).

142. In the case of tenancy of housing lots and other real estate, the tenant has the right to erect the required buildings, in accordance with the contract, and to apply for the construction permit. The lease of a building lot in a zoning area (which in practice is a rarity) must be registered with the municipal judge for real estate affairs. The tenancy can be used as security, as collateral for a loan, and transferred to third parties without the consent of the landlord. The transfer of other categories of land is more restricted, but as a rule transfer is permitted unless there is clear prohibition in the lease contract. Rights concerning lease of land can be registered in the register of mortgages in order to maintain the validity of the contract in the case of conveyance of the ownership of land under tenancy. Contracts of lease can be entered for several specific purposes; for instance, water areas can be leased for fishery, land for mining activities and private or State forests, for forestry or hunting. These possibilities are largely used due to the fact that all natural resources belong to land property and therefore are subject to contract with interested users.

4. Freedom of Acquisition

143. In case an area has been acquired by sale involving conditions on land development, the contract usually refers to a planned land-use which grants or is supposed to grant a certain amount of building rights. Since the amount of a building right depends on public law (plan provision), the contract is not valid if it contradicts the plan or other provisions prescribed by public law.

144. There are no restrictions to the acquisition of land for building purposes. Foreign individuals and companies may also buy land and acquire other rights to land.[28] However, a plan provision may presuppose that the plan has a specified developer. This is the case with public administration, traffic areas, hospitals, and more. Should such a property be in the hands of a private individual or private company, it may be transferred on the basis of the plan by compulsory purchase to the municipality or the State; of course, a contractual transfer is also possible.

28. Restrictions concern all land property in the autonomous area of Aland and elsewhere acquisition of shore land for recreation purposes. Permits can be granted under conditions defined by law.

5. Public Law System

145. Zoning and partition of building rights are regulated in the Land-Use and Building Act (LUBA). This act provides mainly for land-use planning, planning and land-use management contracts. The plan may require formation of building lots to registered units (real estate). This part is regulated in the Real Estate Formation Act. Building lots are then regular units of the real estate registry. They can be transferred and mortgaged as security.

146. In practice, all buildings require a building permit. One of the conditions for the grant of a permit is that the project applied for is not in contradiction with detailed land-use plans or the municipal building regulations. Within the framework of the three categories of plans – the regional plan, the general plan, and the municipal or town plan (zoning) – the regional and general plans are usually not detailed enough to define the content and the location of buildings. Thus, those plans usually determine only the areas where buildings are permitted, the minimum sizes of building sites, and eventually the size and use of buildings. In the case of housing and other densely built up areas, regional and general plans are not a satisfactory basis for granting permits. Instead, a detailed town plan is required.[29] This plan is binding in all respects for the contents of a building permit. The most important aspect in building areas is the determination of building rights in relation to each lot. The rules for the content of the town plan do not limit the assignment of building rights. These are determined in the building permit procedure.

147. General planning principles for built-up areas are set by law (LUBA, section 5). The plan determines the location of city blocks between streets and other open areas. In the detailed plan, city blocks are organized as building lots, which again are precisely determined in a further plan called 'lot distribution'. At this stage, the lots are on paper only (plan lots), but the building right is final after the ratification of the town plan and the lot distribution. If the borders of the planned lots are not in line with the already existing real estate structure, the planned lots need to be formed into registry units in a parcelling procedure in accordance with the lot distribution. If a plan lot consists of parts belonging to different real estate, the owner of the largest or most valuable part has the right to redeem the other parts and thus become the only owner of the future registered lot. Registration requires that all parts of the lot are in the hands of the same owner or owners. The owner can be a juristic person. After that, the real estate is finalized (registered lot). Both plan lots (which are not yet real estate but parcels) and registered lots may be transferred and used as security in the same way as registered real estate.

29. Under certain circumstances, the need of a detailed plan may be replaced by an exemption order which is separate from the building permit.

6. Extinction

148. Building rights exist as long as no land-use provision requires changes. The approval of a new modified plan does not have the consequence that existing building rights would be changed or even disappear. The buildings may remain as long as no structural or functional changes occur, such as enlargement or converting a restaurant into a supermarket. Nonetheless, regular improvement is still allowed.

149. The legislation on cultural heritage (Building Protection Act 60/1985) may affect a building right by enacting necessary restrictions on use, restoration or enlargement. Usually such modifications of a building permit do not limit the building right as it has been used. There are, however, situations where a site has not yet been built in accordance with a plan allowing the destruction of the previous building. In that case, if the old building comes under cultural heritage, the expected building right may not be taken into use. Depending on the situation, this may, under certain conditions, imply compensation from the municipality or the State.

150. Contractual building rights are, as mentioned, mostly connected to a land-management contract with the municipality concerning a development area. Those contracts may require that the developer respect a certain timetable and fulfil other conditions. Time limits are relevant partly due to the fact that the municipality itself has certain obligations to fulfil, especially concerning the infrastructure in a zoning area. Negligence on the developer's part may therefore cause the loss of the agreed upon building right.

C. Land-Management Contract

151. Land-management contracts aim at the planning and construction of larger areas which are either undeveloped or have been used for an activity which does not presently exist (i.e., an industry, harbour or railway). According to regular rules, it is the duty of the municipality to create the infrastructure for housing and recreation areas. The land-management contract creates the possibility of transferring these tasks to a developer, more or less as a condition for making use of the building right, which is foreseen as a kind of compensation. The contract – or the later plan – may also require that polluted soil be cleaned up before the commencement of construction works. Thus, the management contract, in essence, has a financial function. The costs involved will in the end fall on the buyers or tenants of houses and apartments.

152. Land-management contracts have an additional function. According to the Land-Use and Planning Act, a municipality is entitled to levy a development fee against the landowners, i.e., those who have been granted building rights in the detailed plan. This development fee covers the costs of installing and maintaining public works on streets and sanitation. The intention here of a land-management contract would be to define the amount to be levied by the municipality against the landowners concerned. Those who do not enter into such a contract have to pay the fee on the basis of a specific calculation criterion.[30] The fee is a levy which is connected to the ownership of land and which has priority over private claims as a statutory lien.

D. *Rural Planting Right*

1. General

153. A rural planting right[31] does not exist as a legal concept or category of property rights. If the land to be cultivated is not property of the farmer, the regular law on land lease will apply to areas acquired from others to be so used.

154. There are two main regulatory systems in relation to cultivation rights. Plant breeding rights are a category of immaterial rights, regulated by the Plant Breeding Rights Act (1279/2009). The right is based on registration and entitles the holder of the registration exclusively to exploit the defined species professionally. Due to globalization of the market, the application may be presented by subjects according to national law as well as international arrangements, especially members and citizens of the Union for the Protection of New Varieties of Plants (UPOV)[32] and the WTO (section 3 of the Act). The plant species board acts as the national authority for registrations. The registrations are collected in the plant species register. The application must include a description of the differences between the new and existing species. It must also not be available on the market.

155. The content of the breeding right is in line with the general principles concerning immaterial rights. The consent of the holder of the right is required for most categories of economic use, especially production, redevelopment, marketing, export and import, and storage.

2. Farmer's Rights

156. The registered right does not limit the use by others for objectives other than professional purposes, for experiments, or for development and research. A farmer may also use on his own cultivations a sowing seed which he has developed from the species. The law defines additional permitted uses of harvests produced on farms (section 6c of the Act), but the holder of the registered right is entitled to compensation.

---

30. See, e.g., the decision Supreme Administrative Court KHO 2004:87/21.9.2004.
31. Cf. 'emphyteusis' in Roman law. In historical times, there was a system in Finland where farmers had a permanent possession of their land which was property of others. This system caused social problems due to the small size of the holdings and the economic dependence of the holders on the landlords. The system was abolished in the beginning of the twentieth century.
32. The International UPOV is an intergovernmental organization with headquarters in Geneva (Switzerland).

157. The owner of the plant species usually gives contractual rights to use the registered item. The contracting party may not transfer the right to third parties unless this has been explicitly agreed. However, a compulsory right to use a registered plant species may be granted by the court to a professional user in cases where the holder of the right does not open the market for the product, and there are no acceptable reasons for his refusal to do so. There are requirements concerning the entitlement to obtain a compulsory right as well as the modes of using the species. The right may be cancelled at a later stage.

3. CAP

158. The other legal sector of planting regulations refers to the European CAP (EC Regulation No. 1782/2003),[33] according to which community aid may be granted to farms under specific conditions. To this scheme, Finland has added a national subsidy system for areas where the agricultural conditions are, for climate and geographical reasons, demanding. The CAP has been transposed by the Farm Subsidy Act (557/2005) and the Decree of the Council of State on the enforcement of the payment system (758/2005).

159. The aforesaid CAP Regulation provides rules concerning eligibility for receiving community payment (Article 33). According to these rules, farmers will have access to the single payment scheme if, for instance, they have been granted a payment in the reference period of the CAP, or they have received the holding or part of the holding by way of actual or anticipated inheritance, from a farmer who met the prescribed conditions. Payment entitlements may be granted either based on the general area or due to special conditions. Farmers may use the parcels as payment areas for any agricultural activity except permanent crops and certain other products. Thus, the payment is not bound to production; there are also set aside entitlements.

160. The EC legislator emphasizes the importance of connecting the payment scheme to the fulfilment of environmental requirements (cross compliance, Regulation Article 3): a farmer receiving direct payments must respect the statutory management requirements referred to in Annex III, according to the timetable fixed in that Annex and the good agricultural and environmental condition established under Article 5 of the Regulation. The competent national authority must provide the farmer with the list of statutory management requirements and good agricultural and environmental conditions to be respected. Member States shall also ensure that all agricultural land, especially land which is no longer used for production purposes, is maintained in good agricultural and environmental condition.

33. Council Regulation (EC) No. 1782/2003 of 29 Sep. 2003 establishing common rules for direct support schemes under the common agricultural policy.

161. Member States must define, at national or regional level, minimum requirements for good agricultural and environmental conditions on the basis of the framework set up in Annex IV, taking into account the specific characteristics of the areas concerned, including soil and climatic condition, existing farming systems, land-use, crop rotation, farming practices, and farm structures. This is without prejudice to the standards governing good agricultural practices as applied in the context of Council Regulation (EC) No. 1257/1999 and to agri-environment measures applied above the reference level of good agricultural practices.

162. Each Member State must set up an integrated administration and control system. Elements of the integrated system are (a) a computerized data base; (b) an identification system for agricultural parcels; (c) a system for the identification and registration of payment entitlements; (d) aid applications; (e) an integrated control system; and (f) a single system to record the identity of each farmer who submits an aid application.

163. According to Finnish regulations, the applicant must have possessed the holding for which he applies for payment entitlements on 28 April 2006. Ownership, rural lease, possession based on will, and corresponding documents are accepted as titles of possession. If payment is applied for livestock production without arable land, the activity has to be run at the said date. An environmental permit serves as an example of proof for such an activity.

III. Rights of Additional Floors, Building and Sub-building

164. The concept of 'floor' is relevant to construction law and especially in relation to detailed planning (LUBA, Chapter 16). A land-use plan may assign, in addition to the area of building rights, a number of admissible floors. For this reason, it is necessary to define to what extent spaces in a building are not 'floors' but instead basements, including parking area, or attic space. Characteristics for a floor are that the area is located mainly over the surface line of the building lot and appear as a part of the front facade of the building. Opening other areas in a house to be used in connection with other floors may require that basement or attic spaces be converted and assigned to be treated as 'floors'. This may be the case in connection with reconstructions.

165. In urban areas where floors are determined by a detailed plan and the maximum number has already been used, such a new assignment usually requires the amendment of the (zoning) plan or an exception granted by the municipality. Restructuring of attics into habitation space is presently a popular way for habitation companies to collect resources for repairs. The right to realize attic housing is often sold to construction enterprises or other interested investors, but private persons may also buy attic building rights and, hence, obtain shares in the habitation or other company. The plan usually includes the condition that the reconstruction does not affect the appearance of the building.

166. Also the creation of 'real' additional floors is possible. In planning areas, where there is no important cultural value, an amended plan may allow for complementary building in existing 'gaps'. Otherwise, adding of floors is submitted to the general rules of discretion according to the LUBA (Chapter 7). Additional floors are legally part of the existing building. If it is jointly owned by a share company, an added building right usually increases the number of shares in the company. Depending on the situation, the habitation company may retain the shares relating to the added floors for later purposes or sell them out to someone who becomes a shareholder in the company.

167. 'Sub-building' is a technical term, which refers to the use of the surface. Buildings, especially commercial buildings and city centres, may have space without direct access to the outside of the building. There are also sub-buildings without a functional connection to the building on the surface. This is the case especially for shelters, areas connecting subways, and parking lots. If the latter spaces are not property of the real estate in question, the operators or constructors have to apply for possession of the space before initiating works. The legal basis for an independent sub-building is usually a zoning plan. Such a plan partly entitles the operator to carry out the project – other entitlements and permits may also be necessary – and partly it serves as a title for compulsory taking of the space belonging to someone else. Where sub-buildings are connected to the land use of the surface estate, the discretion of allowing additional floors (parking, stores) underground is part of the permit procedure under the guidance of detailed planning and local building regulations.[34] There is no general restriction against adding sub-buildings to buildings, other than those relating to planning and technical safety.

168. In the case of independent sub-buildings, i.e., which are not covered by a surface construction project, a detailed plan may be drafted to serve as guidance for the realization. A plan is usually required when the owner of the real estate is not the planner of the project. Legally, separate sub-buildings, for example, shelters, storage areas, traffic service areas, have their origin in a usufruct or compulsory right (eventually easement) burdening the real estate because the legislation does not recognize three-dimensional property units. The title to this space may be transferred to others in the same manner as movable property.

§3. Leasehold Interests: Chattels Real

169. Land lease involves several types of tenancy according to the Land Lease Act (258/1966). In order to avoid permanent possession of tenants, all tenancy has a limited duration. If possession of land continues after the end of the ultimate limit set by law, the lease expires unless a new contract has been concluded. The categories of tenancy are lease of a lot in a zoning area, lease of other real estate for housing, lease of rural and agricultural land, and, additionally, lease of land not mentioned (e.g., a vacant area for storage of waste or excavation of resources). The

34. LUBA ss 135–136.

maximum duration of a lease is 100 years. If land is leased for the erection of buildings, the duration should not be less than thirty years.

170. The Finnish system, originating from continental European tradition, does not incorporate the common law concepts of legal and equitable interests. An interest in land and real property usually presupposes a right, based on a deed in accordance with legal requirements. Only in a few cases, possession or factual tradition may be used as arguments to prove the existence of a legal interest. The main presumption of law is that a registered owner has full title in the property. Third parties' interests or rights in a property may be based on legally performed procedures or transactions (contract of use, lease, easement, etc.). These positions implying limited interest in a property, owned by others, are mostly regulated by law. Oral contracts are valid *inter partes* in some cases, especially in the case of leases of house and land. In some situations of land-use, oral consents may be binding for subsequent owners, on the basis of habit or equity (e.g., consent to tolerate nuisance from a neighbouring property).

§4. Limited Property Rights

171. The system of rights to property other than ownership consists of different categories of limited or special rights. The rights can be divided in two categories, namely those which are established for a person and those which are based on the relationship between property units. Main rights in the first category are usufruct and security to which the property is legally related, e.g., by agreement or registration. The second category includes principally the rights established by an authority to serve one real estate unit over the other – mostly referred to as easement. The principle of *numerus clausus* was earlier supported in the sense that usufructs could be valid in defined cases only. The range of usufruct agreements has however developed, and there is no need to limit the forms of legally valid arrangements. Therefore, the categories of acceptable special rights are not determined by law. In fact, recent social and economic development favours the adoption of new categories (leasing and factoring).

172. The *numerus clausus* principle appears in some legal contexts, especially in cases of easements (servitude) based on land survey to secure the viability of neighbouring land units. But law often allows contractual deviations from the legal categories, which may then be adopted as part of the authoritative decision (contractual easements; e.g., allocation of joint areas, roads and service buildings).

§5. Lease of Land

I. General Remarks

173. Land tenancy has a contractual basis and is regulated by law (Land Tenancy Act 258/1966). Historically, before the beginning of the twentieth century, land tenancy did not sufficiently take into account the rights and interests of the tenants. The supremacy of landowners created to a certain extent a social class of tenants, who were, in practice, dependent on the decisions of the landowners concerning living conditions of the tenants and their families. Contractual equity and release from the burden of tenancy opened the way for tenants to become, through special legislation on redemption of rented land, owners of the land they inhabited or cultivated (land reform). Occasionally, laws were enacted to support redemption of leased land by the tenants. At present, land tenancy is based on the principle of freedom of contract. The duration of a contract is basically limited, depending on the category of lease. Both parties must also respect the rules on the right to notice. This rule of contractual freedom also allows contracts of land-use which are not properly under the land tenancy rules; instead, general contractual law applies (e.g., occupancy of land for forestry, water management, or mining).

174. The present Land Tenancy Act has its deficiencies as it was mainly enacted for rural areas. Reforms were attempted over the years but until now no new legislation has been achieved. The act takes into account the principles of contract law as adopted in the Contracts Act or refers to the provisions and principles in this act. This means, for instance, that a tenancy or its content can be adjusted due to unreasonable terms or later development of contractual conditions (Contract Act section 36).

175. The Land Tenancy Act is generic by nature and applies to all land tenancy situations. Thus, there is no distinction between leases of private land and property of the State, municipalities or congregations. Public land may, however, be rented for specific purposes as housing or for industrial activities. The lease of private land seems not to be commonly used for housing and industry. There are, in addition, some provisions in the game and fisheries legislation on land rent for corresponding special needs of these activities. The Land Tenancy Act applies to leases of land, including buildings. If a building only is under lease, the Habitation Rent Act (481/1995) is applicable.[35] As rentable land or other property is not registered, statistical information is not available.

176. In addition to general rules, the Land Tenancy Act provides provisions on specific categories of land leases. The provisions of the act vary to some extent depending on the purpose of the lease. In relation to housing areas two categories are recognized, namely, leases of residential property or land for habitation and agreements for the lease of building lots (similar to ground rent, see paragraph 194 below). Further categories are leases of agricultural land and – as a supplement to the mentioned categories – leases of land for other purposes. Leases of land for habitation are the most common category of land leases.

35. House rent may comprise a not remarkable part of annexed land, for instance a parking lot or a small garden.

II. General Rules

177. The Land Tenancy Act provides rules which are either mandatory, because they are aimed to protect the tenant, or voluntary, depending on the agreement between the parties. A lease contract should usually be in writing, and terms other than those included in the contract are not legally binding. The duration of the lease period depends on the category of lease. For lease of residential land the maximum duration of a lease contract is 100 years. If the area needs to be built by the tenant, the minimum duration of a contract is thirty years. The buildings erected by the tenant are usually the tenant's property. Leases of agricultural land may be agreed to be valid for fifteen years and, if not otherwise agreed, endure for a minimum of two years.

178. The mutual obligations of the parties are prescribed by law. The landlord's main obligation is to deliver the land in the possession of the tenant without interference by third parties (creditors or successors of the landlord). Again the tenant has to pay the agreed rent and to take care of the object. His right to use resources or to erect buildings depends on the contract and on the category of lease. His right to extend the lease further without the consent of the lessor may also be limited.

179. Grounds for the landowner's notice to terminate during the validity of a lease contract are stipulated by law. If the contract was concluded for a limited period, no notice is required to end the lease after that period. The tenant has no right to claim continuation of a contract.

III. Urban Land Lease

180. The Land Tenancy Act does not in its general part concerning lease of land make a distinction between urban and rural land. Therefore planning law or municipal statutory regulations does not affect the contractual situation concerning leases of land. The content of the lease contract may, of course, take into account the specific conditions which as examples, zoning, infrastructure and more may cause in urban areas. But this is not a legal prerequisite of the contract itself. Under the Land Tenancy Act two categories are related to urban land, namely ground rent (see paragraph 194 below) and lease of housing land.

A. *Special Statutory Provisions*

181. Lease of housing land is a category of land lease (Land Tenancy Act, Chapter 3) and the subject may be either urban or agricultural land. The land is appointed in the lease contract to serve as a building lot for the tenant. The lot may already be equipped with buildings or the tenant can obtain the right by contract to erect his own buildings.[36] The duration of such a contract is limited in time with a maximum of 100 years. If the tenant has the right to build the minimum duration is thirty years. Also, if no duration has been agreed upon the duration is thirty years.

B. Content of the Right

182. Unless otherwise agreed in the contract, the lease title gives authority to the tenant to transfer the leasehold to a third party without the consent of the landlord. In this case the lease is also hereditable and can be bequeathed by will. The holder of the lease is liable to apply for registration of the lease in the land property register if the lease is transferable to a third party and if the leaseholder is given the right to erect buildings for the use of land (REC Chapter 14 section 2). The regular time limit for the application is six months after entering the contract or the transfer of the lease.

183. Lease of a housing lot implies the obligation to erect buildings according to the zoning plan. On the other hand, an ongoing activity on leased land does not prevent the adoption of a new land-use plan which determines the area for a different mode of use.[37]

C. Mandatory Prorogation of Housing Lease

184. The lease contract may include a restriction of the tenant's right to transfer the lease. Such a clause does not prevent, in case of death of the tenant, the surviving spouse or direct heirs from continuing the contract lease, if they so wish. Such a wish should be forwarded to the landlord within three months after the death of the tenant.

D. Registration

185. Registration follows the general rules of the Real Estate Code (Chapter 14): all land tenancy contracts may be registered in order to make them binding against successors of the owner and his successors or creditors. Registration is mandatory if the tenant intends to transfer his right and if the lease involves the right to erect buildings. Otherwise and especially when the landlord has provided the required buildings, registration is not mandatory.

---

36. Right to building on leased land could be separated in execution (Supreme Court KKO 2003:2/ 2.2.2004).
37. Supreme Administrative Court KHO 2009:63/23.6.2009.

E. Extinction

186. Regular rules concerning extinction of the lease apply to a housing lease as well. In addition, if building has been convened to be performed within a period of time and the tenant fails to fulfil this obligation, the landowner may give notice within one month after the end of that period.

187. When the rent period terminates, the relations between tenant and landowner will be settled. If the tenant has built, in accordance with the contract, buildings for housing, the landowner shall redeem them, unless it has otherwise been agreed. Other constructions are not covered by this ruling.

IV. Rural Lease

188. The categories relating to rural areas are rent of habitation land (other than ground rent) and of farming land, with or without necessary buildings. If land is rented for purposes other than habitation or farming (e.g., for recreation, fishery, etc.), certain more simple rules apply. Lease of agricultural land has been a rather common way to increase the area of the cultivator's own farm, e.g., in order to make industry more viable or to fulfil the requirements of receiving State subsidy. The main purpose of the lease is to provide additional field area for small farms. The Act also provides for specific rules on tenants' rights and obligations concerning existing and new constructions and equipment. More simple provisions apply if the lease concerns agricultural land without buildings. For improvements on land or constructions, the tenant may claim compensation only if this has been agreed upon.

A. Special Statutory Provisions

189. Farming land may be leased with (farm) or without buildings (agricultural land). A farm may consist of one or more or parcels. A farm is not a category of property units, rather a term of agriculture. Therefore there are no limits for leasing farm land in terms of property rights. A farm (with buildings) may be rented for a maximum of fifteen years. The lease term for other agricultural land is limited to a maximum of ten years, but the duration also depends on the cultivation season. If the term endures for more than two years, a written contract is required.

B. Content of the Right

190. A lease gives possession of the land for farming purposes which is eventually defined by contract. The tenant may not, if not agreed, transfer his right to third parties. The Tenancy Act provides rules concerning tenant's buildings and the use of existing buildings on the farm. If buildings have been erected in conformity with the lease, the landowner may be obliged to redeem these objects at the end of the lease term. The tenant may also receive compensation for improvement or investments on the farm. A crop which matures after the lease term, as a rule is property of the tenant who sowed it.

C. *Mandatory Prorogation of Housing Lease*

191. What was said above about urban lease applies to farm land as well. In a reorganization of real estate (re-allotment or expropriation), the rented land may become part of a property not owned by the landlord; a mediation aiming at the continuation of the lease between the tenant and the new owner should be attained. If this is not possible, the land survey officer may rule that the lease will prevail. If this causes prejudice to the owner, the lease may also be declared annulled.

D. *Registration*

192. Registration follows the general rules of the Real Estate Code (Chapter 14): lease contracts may be registered to protect the tenant against successors and other claims concerning the property, but not restrictions based on public law, for instance zoning.

E. *Annulment*

193. Since a lease is valid for a limited period of time, the lease ends with the expiration of the term without further action. Premature termination of a lease requires notice which is possible for both sides through conditions prescribed by law. These grounds are mandatory as far as the landlord is concerned (Act, section 21): the common situation is related to negligence of the tenant in fulfilling his obligations. The landlord may also require compensation for his losses due to the termination of the lease.

§6. Rent Charge

I. Ground Rents: Concept and Classes

194. There is one peculiar category concerning the lease of a building lot on detailed planned areas (Land Tenancy Act Chapter 2). The so-called lease of a building lot or ground rent has a specific function and does not, therefore, prevent parties from concluding a regular lease contract for the same or similar urban areas. Ground rent is regulated in the Land Tenancy Act and, therefore, ranges under the rules of a lease. Nonetheless, a so-called ground rent represents a legally strong ground for possession and is, therefore, close to permanent right of use of urban land. The intention is to grant the tenant a rather independent position vis-à-vis the landowner as far as the use of building rights and transfer of the lease are concerned. However, Finnish law does not recognize unlimited periods of possession to holders of titles other than owners (e.g., *emphyteusis*). The duration of the ground rent may vary from thirty to one hundred years. If the rent appears to be unreasonable, it may be adjusted in accordance with the general rules concerning lease of the Contracts Act (section 36).

195. In order to attain the consequences stipulated by law, the tenant has to apply for registration of his right, which is basically in the same order as provided for registration of mortgage. A lease contract concerning a building lot can be entered in the property register only if the real estate is a building lot according to a valid detailed plan.[38] The rent contract covers such a real estate as a whole. A contract may be registered only if the lease contract fulfils the prescribed requirements, especially in writing and an expressed will to enter a lease qualified as ground rent. In addition, the property must not be encumbered with a mortgage or other deficiencies attributable to the owner, for instance execution.

196. The lease rent of a building lot itself may serve as mortgageable property of the tenant. As a rule, all constructions and works existing or initiated during the lease are covered by the contract. This means that the tenant acts as the proprietor of buildings and other investments during the duration of the lease.

II. Constitution and Characters

197. The lease of a building lot (ground rent) requires, in addition to the lease contract, registration in order to obtain its legal status. Other categories of land lease may be registered if the tenant intends to protect his right against third parties, especially successors of the owner. But without registration, the tenant is protected according to the Land Tenancy Act against certain claims from third parties.

III. Extinction

198. After the termination of the rent period, the landowner is obliged to redeem immovable property with some exceptions. In other lease contracts, this duty is not compulsory. The ground rent contract of a building lot may be renewed before the end of the lease period; in this case, all rights and duties invested in the lease of the building do not cease but remain as they were when established and registered. The renewal in practice has the effect that, if the parties so wish, the ground rent has an indefinite and eventually permanent duration.

38. See Real Estate Formation Act, ss 34–35 and above 139–142.

§7. USE AND HABITATION

I. Concept, Statutory Provisions, and General Features

199. A contract on a room or a house rent is regulated by the House Rent Act (481/1995). The Act applies to rent on all buildings and apartments for habitation by contract between the owner and the tenant. The Act does not apply to professional lodging firms. Additional or separate rules apply to the rental of municipal and State-financed habitations. A rent contract may stipulate duration until further notice or for a limited period of time.

200. A term limiting the tenant's right to apply for registration of his right for security is not valid. The tenant whose right is registered has priority against others claiming possession of the apartment. If the object has been rented twice, the tenant who in good faith takes possession of the apartment has priority, and the other candidate is entitled to require compensation from the landlord. If a married couple shares an apartment, they are both liable for the rent. In an instance where the apartment – as well as a building or share in a habitation company – is sold, the conveyee is under certain conditions bound by the rent agreement.

201. The Act provides rules concerning the amount and payment of the rent, the settlement of disputes, and the mutual obligations of the parties, as well as the grounds for the landlord to give notice. In principle, the tenant requires the consent of the landlord if he wants to transfer his rights to someone else. Subtenancy is specifically regulated in order to give the subtenant protection in relation to the tenant and his successors.

202. Employment housing is defined as a category of tenancy where the tenant is a firm or other employer who offers the apartment or building to be used by the personnel as habitation. The contract is concluded between the landlord and the employer, not the person taking the object in possession. The rights of the resident are, in terms of actions, limited compared to a tenant who has entered the contract in his own name.

203. Separate legislation deals with rent of commercial space (Act 482/1995). This Act applies to a building or a part of it to be used for other purposes than habitation. The contract may include in addition to the building or apartment also the parcel's location. A rent is either limited to a fixed term or valid until further notice. A contract must be in writing; if not the validity is assumed to last until further notice. The rules concerning mediation of unreasonable terms, competing contracts, and use of security are basically the same as in the rent of habitation. However, the tenant may more freely dispose of the business premises; for instance, in the case of subtenancy to other merchants, possession of up to half of the object may be given to someone else without the landlord's consent. If he transfers his right to another merchant as part of a business sale, the landlord must be informed of this. The regular period of notice of termination for contracts concluded until further notice is three months.

204. A term limiting the tenant's right to register his right for permanence is void. In the case of public auction, the buyer of the property may give six months notice on the rental contract. In cases of voluntary conveyance of the property, the rent contract remains valid under certain conditions, especially when the tenant has taken possession of the premises, the rent is included in the sale contract, or the tenant has registered his right. The mutual obligations of the parties include liability for damage, delay and compensation.

II. Constitution and Extinction

205. A lease contract shall be concluded in writing, especially if the rent is supposed to have a limited duration. If the contract for some reason does not exist in writing, the rent is enforceable until further notice. In the case of rental of a leisure apartment, the contract may also be an oral one. A security deposit equal up to the rent of three months may be required. If no duration has been agreed upon, the rent terminates when the parties agree or give notice on grounds provided by law.

206. Grounds for terminating a rent term before the end of the contractual period are provided in law. Ultimately, notice may be given in cases of negligence in fulfilling the contractual or legal obligations. In some cases, a measure of public law (expropriation, public auction, etc.) may create grounds for annulling the contract. Bankruptcy of the tenant is also a ground for annulling the contract unless the landlord has received satisfactory security.

§8. Easement and Profit

I. Concept, Classes, and Features

207. An easement (servitude) is defined as a legal relationship of use between two pieces of real estate or other registered units. Thus, one of the objects is serving (*servience*) the other (*dominance*). On both sides, several units may be related to one easement. Easements mainly have two legal bases, one in the legislation of survey, the other in the law on construction. Characteristically, easements are confirmed or are established by authoritative decisions, and in most cases, they are also registered in the land register or in another information data system. In addition to this, the distinction compared to usufruct is that the entitled party is usually a person who may register his right in order to gain protection against the rights or claims of third parties. Usufruct does not require registration (mortgage) in order to be valid *inter partes*.

208. Easements, explicitly so-called in legal sources, are constituted mainly in survey procedures or in connection to the location of buildings in zoning areas. The law defines 'rights to use', not 'easements', as situations where limited rights have been established according to water, mining, and road legislation. For instance, a water construction project may cause the loss of a functioning well or other water intake. The holder of such a permit is, if required, obliged to organize a replacement water system for those who need it (Water Act, 587/2011, Chapter 12 section 15). Likewise, if such a project cuts off a passage crossing a watercourse or its ice cover, replacement of certain modes of transportation should be established. In these and comparable cases, the parties may conclude a contract which is then also included in the authority's decision. Finally, limited rights based on the Expropriation Act fall under this definition.

209. If defined as a relationship between registered units, an easement as a permanent burden for one and an entitlement for another unit is distinguished under the rule of *numerus clausus*: easements cannot be established beyond the criteria stated by law. On the other hand, the legal system recognizes certain categories of 'rights of use' which indeed are established to serve land units as well. In order to facilitate land-use projects (roads, water constructions, etc.), an authority may prescribe entitlements and restrictions between land units. The main difference compared to an easement is that the entitled party usually is a land-use project, not necessarily a registered unit. However, the legal condition for establishment and the rules for registration are similar to those concerning easements. Since the rights are related to projects, they may be either temporary or permanent, whereas easements usually are permanent by nature. The legislation on expropriation also recognizes the creation of 'special rights' to burden real estate or to restrict its use in favour of a project based on a public need (see paragraph 483). Therefore, the difference between road easements and expropriation of land for road purposes is, in the case of public roads, rather slight. The right to enter private roads is classified as an 'easement' or 'right to road' which is an equivalent term.

210. There is a distinction between contractual easements and compulsory easements. In both cases, the easement must satisfy the legal characteristics of an easement. The particular difference appears in cases where there is no real requirement for the entitled real estate to acquire an easement. The constitution of an easement presupposes consent or a contract with the owner of the serving land unit before the authority makes the decision concerning the establishment.

II. Profit

211. Rights to profit may be established on a contractual basis. Common areas applied are forest and soil resources. The right to profit is usually connected to the possession of land and water as long as the product in question has not been separated from its origin. If the right has been established in favour of someone as a usufruct, he has right to the profit as soon as it has been separated in accordance with the contract. Certain categories of usufructs may be registered in order to become binding against third parties. In certain situations, it may be difficult to decide whether the possessor of land is entitled to use the profit or whether it belongs to the owner. Usually the possessor (i.e., tenant) is entitled to use the amount of profit corresponding to the growth during his period of possession. In instances of non-renewable resources, the extent of use may be limited to domestic use.

212. The taking of resources and use of the profits may also be the content of easements in which case the right follows the title of the real estate.

III. Subjects and Objects

213. The literature recognizes easements in relation to real estate and personal easements. As stated before, parties to easements are land units and not usually persons. Nevertheless, in some cases an easement, by nature, may serve the owner, for instance, of real estate for his lifetime or an otherwise defined context which is not transferable to the next owner. The difference in relation to usufruct is that the service is offered by a land unit, not a person. If the easement is not personal, it follows the ownership or possession of the entitled property. Unlike usufructs, easements are not registrable in the property register (mortgaging the owner's right), but instead they are constituted in the land register, referring to both concerned register units as parties to the easement.

214. The most typical of these property rights are legally easements (servitudes) which may be to grant one parcel of real estate the right to pass through a road, to a water area, or to use in one way or other the land or resources of another property. In addition, specific laws on waters, roads, mines and expropriation may acknowledge categories of specific property rights other than those explicitly enumerated as easements in the Real Estate Formation Act (REFA, 554/1995). These other rights of use may either give full possession of an area or a limited utilization of sites or resources (e.g., location of constructions to support bridge or dam).

IV. Constitution

215. Easement is above defined as a physical relationship between real estate and other registered units. In order to improve the management of real estate, a permanent easement may be established in favour of one real estate to burden another registered unit for a set of defined purposes (REFA, section 154). The purposes of permanent easements are:

(1) to catchments of domestic water use;
(2) to conduct water and to allocate water mains and equipments for the use of water for domestic use;
(3) to conduct water for drainage of land;
(4) to locate sanitation pipes and connected equipments and constructions for conducting sewage water into a ditch or a watercourse;
(5) to locate and use cables for telephone, electric, gas, energy and other sources and to locate related equipments and constructions;
(6) for land for parking of cars, keeping boats, a dock, swimming place, storage, and loading for timber;
(7) necessary adjacent land for fishery;
(8) place to take stone, sand, turf, and other resources for domestic purposes;

(9) appropriate space for location and use of constructions for civil defence;
(10) location and use of heating systems and waste treatment facilities;
(11) connection of ways to public roads in zoning areas.

V. Content of the Right

216. If the need is temporary or the conditions for establishing an easement permanently are not suitable, an easement may be granted exceptionally for a limited period of time. The servitudes are usually created in the same procedure where real estate parcels are formed (survey) but the rights may also be determined in a separate survey procedure. Duration and other clauses for the use of easements may be determined in the same procedure or later in a review procedure. An easement serves the units for which it has been determined. If the entitled real estate is subsequently partitioned, the easement (for instance, a boat dock or private way) is not automatically available to the new registered unit without a decision in a survey procedure. The survey commission decides which of the partitioned units is entitled to use the easement in question. Eventually, the easement may also be declared available for several or all of the new real estate.

VI. Restrictions and Rules for the Establishment of Real Estate Easements in Planning Areas

217. Essentially, easements in planning zones have two roles, either to function in a traditional manner between lots or to create support for infrastructural measures. If a detailed plan has been drafted for built-up areas on shore, an easement may also be established to satisfy common needs of the real estate (common use area). The easement may encumber one or several lots in the planning area. The consent of the owners is not required since the plan reservation serves as title for the measure (REFA, section 154a).

218. The first rule concerning creation of an easement is that it is based on a contract between the owners of the entitled and encumbered real units, eventually also between the owner and the municipality if it is entitled to obtain easement on private land. An additional condition is that the easement is supposedly not to cause excessive inconvenience to the encumbered unit. Without a contract or consent, an easement may be created in a survey procedure concerning partition or restructuring of real estate which creates the need of new easements or the alteration of existing ones. In such situations, it is also mandatory to arrange passage for each registered unit to a road for which an easement may be created. The survey commission decides the site of encumbrance and the conditions for the entitlement to use the easement.

219. According to the Water Act 2011, an easement may be established entitling real estate to locate a water or sewage pipe in the ground of other real estate

(Chapter 4 section 8). This right is created by the decision of the water permit authority in accordance with the Water Act. The condition for establishing such an easement is the need of an easement to locate pipes and equipments on an individual's land or water area. Similar provisions are found in the Land-Use Planning and Building Act, which provides for the location of all varieties of pipes, cables, and other municipal constructions on another estate as easement. Here the decision is made by the municipal building authority. Conditions for creating such a right are the same as in the Water Act.

220. In addition, further titles of use between interrelated real estate may be based on the Expropriation Act if there is a public need and if the law allows the taking. The same applies to numerous situations of land-use management as regulated in the LUBA, the Public Roads Act, the Private Roads Act, the Aviation Act, and the Nature Conservation Act. In these cases, compulsory rights mostly entitle the applicant to use a property of another in a specific manner. In this sense the content and conditions of granting a right are similar to the regulatory system of creating easements. A specific right may, however, go further than an easement as the project in question determines what kinds of rights are necessary. Projects may, for instance, require artificial changes of the normal water level, which may affect building rights, agriculture, and other positions. In other situations, compulsory rights may lead to the extinction or limitation of existing rights. Depending on the legislation, the precondition of granting a specific right is either public need (a general condition for measures of expropriation) or a comparable importance to carry out a project. The rights and comparable limitations may contribute not only to economic land-use but also to protection of nature and other sites. In all cases, full compensation is foreseen to the transferor of forfeited property rights.

VII. Easements for Buildings

221. Building easements are a category that is regulated in the Land-Use and Planning Act. These easements are established to serve buildings, not registered units, and are therefore under the management rules of building law. By definition, a building easement serves a building lot or a building to permanent use of another building (LUBA, section 158). The formal requirement is a contract between the owners of the concerned building lots. The municipal building authority decides upon the creation of such an easement and that there is a need and that the inconvenience to the encumbered unit is not unreasonable. Certain public needs provided in a detailed plan (civil shelter, a passage between buildings, the support of constructions, etc.) may be established under the same conditions but without a contract between the parties involved.

VIII. Extinction

222. An easement may be relocated, or amended conditions may be prescribed if the parties concerned agree or give their consent. The amendment takes place in a survey procedure. In certain important conditions, the change may be decided without a contract or consent of the parties. Under certain circumstances, an easement may have to be established for a limited time only.

223. An easement may be abolished if the land-use conditions have changed to the extent that the easement is no longer necessary. A necessary easement may be abolished if the inconvenience to the encumbered real estate proves to be excessive, and the harm can be diminished by relocating the easement. Increased detrimental impact caused by a change of an easement shall be compensated by the owner of the real estate profiting from the harmful easement.

§9. Licenses

224. Use of land often requires a permit of an authority. Usufruct and easement do not solely entitle an activity if there is an additional need for a permit or a planning provision. Grounds for licensing are found in numerous acts, especially the Planning and Building Act, the road legislation, the Environmental Protection Act, the Water Act, the Soil Resources Act, and more. If the use would affect the neighbourhood physically (building beyond the limits of the site), the consent of the neighbour may be required as well. The rule is that public law and the need for permits cannot be set aside by consents from neighbours, or even municipalities and authorities. On the other hand, owners or possessors of land and water areas are usually entitled to use the resources without a license as long as the use is limited to domestic purposes (right to basic use). In principle, there is no legal guarantee for getting a permit or license (e.g., building license). The discretion of the authorities is defined by law; thus, there is no voluntary or political discretion over the suitability of planned projects.

225. The constitutional protection of property rights (Constitution 2000 section 15) does not, according to legal practice, guarantee more than the right to 'basic use',[39] which means that to an excessive extent, a permit can be rejected without constitutional doubts. This rule applies to general restrictions based on law and is, therefore, not necessarily applicable in all cases. If, for instance, the reason for rejection of the permit is the protection of a natural site or some other selective measure demanding restriction of land-use, the rejection may have the nature of expropriation and instigates the duty of the society to pay compensation.

226. If the application for a permit is denied on legal grounds, e.g., for health and safety or nature values, the society does not usually pay the compensation, but there may be some exception here, especially in building law. Should the rejection of the application follow from a detailed plan, compensation may be due only if the plan is proved to be unreasonable for the landowner.

227. In certain situations, the use of land or resources requires a license in the sense that the applicant is expected to fulfil additional qualifications for acquiring

39. In terms of constructions and use of resources the concept is too vague for setting clear criteria.

the title. For example, this applies to mining law (Mining Act 621/2011). In principle, from a constitutional point of view, minerals belong to the owner of the land. However, he has no right to profit from the resource on a contractual basis, and, therefore, is not entitled to choose the mining operator. Instead, mining activities require a license granted by the administration (Ministry of Employment and Trade). The applicant may be any corporate body registered in the European Community or a Finnish natural person. The authority will study the economic basis for the activity applied for as well as the expertise and solidity of the applicant. The first stage of licensing covers research of the appointed site without the right to exploit the resource economically; the second stage appoints the essential mining area for exploitation. During this action, the landowner is entitled to receive partial compensation for the use of his property and resources as well as an annual fee as profit.

228. One category of license is the right to carry out research and production in accordance with the Gene Technology Act (377/1995). This legislation transposes the corresponding directives of the European Community. The legislation serves several objectives, primarily human safety, environmental risk management, and liability. Certain modes of gene technological activities require a permit (license), while others must be notified to the competent authority. A license may be granted for a contained use after an investigation of the impacts and risks of the activity. According to the amended EC legislation, a license is also required for the deliberate release of genetically modified organisms. Here the competent authority is the Board of Gene Technology within the Ministry of Social Security and Health.

§10. RESTRICTIVE COVENANTS

229. Restrictive covenants may be entered between holders of titles, especially with the owners and possessors, and a public authority. The aim of such covenants is largely to generate protection of natural sites or cultural buildings. According to the Nature Conservation Act, private preservation areas may be established based either on the application of the landowner or on the prescription of the competent authority. The conditions of the protection are set by law, but the competent authority and landowner may to some extent assemble the content of the measures in the named preservation. For instance, housing and farming may be allowed at a determined site, but the use of other natural resources may be limited. Also, based on nature protection programmes, voluntary agreements on natural preserves are practiced, especially in order to protect biological diversity in natural forests. The State may, in return for voluntary restrictions, give compensation to the owners.

230. Moreover, in the context of EC law, covenants occur. Farmers have to restrict the effluents from agriculture in accordance with the Directive 91/676 on the protection of waters from pollution by nitrates. Eutrophication is a remarkable threat to waters also beyond the area of that Directive. For this reason, the national water programme policy supports voluntary measures to limit the impact of fertilizers and pesticides, partly in order to prevent further eutrophication of the Baltic Sea. The measures to be taken and the restrictions to be applied (good agricultural practice) are in these cases based on covenants. Large units require a permit for the production and for emissions.

231. A third example of restrictive covenants is cultural protection. The Building Protection Act (60/1985) provides rules on protection of historical and cultural buildings and sites. Detailed plan regulations are also used to enforce restrictions in order to protect buildings against demolition or destruction. The specialized act usually applies in the case of individually protected sites, whereas plan provisions serve larger areas, e.g., blocks. Protection covers the fixture as well. Also, depending on the situation, a part of a building or only the fixture may be protected. In addition to buildings, other constructions, e.g., bridges, wells, small parks, are suitable objects if they are related to the building and its close surroundings.

232. The decision as to what extent preservation is required and admissible is legally bound by law, but often additional covenants between the competent authority and the possessor of the building are reached to define in detail what activities are tolerable and what repairs might be acceptable. But also beyond these areas of legislation, voluntary arrangement may be reached if, for instance, the holder of the site is actively interested in maintaining the present state of the site. The authority or a municipality may then support such an approach by giving the site contractual protection (e.g., a museum).

233. Antiquities are protected under the regime of the corresponding acts (Antiquities Protection Act 295/1963 and the Church Act 1054/1993). Antiquities are either fixed relics or movable relics of antiquity. Wrecks are also protected under the Antiquity Act. The protection of antiquities is based directly on law (prohibition to enter or move) unless the competent authority has given its consent or permit. Movable objects are the same as fixed antiquities if they appear in a functional context, for instance, in a graveyard. Randomly found items should be delivered to authorities. In the regime of these acts, there exists only little space for covenants, but since museum authorities may estimate to what extent protection is necessary, the landowner may be allowed to perform certain activities (digging) if he follows the limits agreed upon. Negotiations are often used in order to avoid situations of total restrictions where the State risks having to pay compensation for excessive restrictions.

Chapter 4. Security Interests

234. Security interests or value rights are, in addition to usufruct, one main category of limited rights. Objects of both immovable and movable property are suitable for providing security to creditors or other supplier of services. The object is usually property of the (financial) debtor, but in some cases, there are also limited rights to property that may serve as security. Securities, within the given literature, are systematized into two groups: proprietary securities and securities under charge. In cases of proprietary security, the creditor is – or remains until further notice – owner of the property. This security is available in case of sale to secure the payment of the purchase price. Proprietary security also includes the categories of security transfer (assignment by way of security) and financial leasing. In these cases, the creditor is the owner of the property under the security. The group of securities under charge covers situations where the debtor is the owner of the security. The main categories here are lien and the pledge and right of retention. Lien is economically the most important category.

235. A further security interest correlates to the relationship between ownership and limited rights. The holder of such a right (lease, extraction right) may register his contractual right, thereby obtaining a guarantee for the existence or continuation of the right when the real estate is conveyed to someone else. Registered rights may also be used as security (ground rent).

236. A group of security rights consists of land charges. This means that a property, usually real estate, is due to pay a charge. These charges have their basis in public law, and the party entitled to collect the charge is often the municipality or its unit (sanitation, roads, waste transportation, survey fees), but also other bodies, such as forest management associations or the state administration. Often these charges fall within the provisions on statutory liens. In civil law, contractual arrangements – for example the sale of real estate – may imply the creation of a regular charge or service in favour of the seller (so-called retired farmer's portion). These situations are borderline between usufruct and lien; theoretically, at least the real estate gives rise to the liability for the performance in the same way as in case of a lien. The nature of the right may be physical (living, cultivation) or monetary (payment).

237. An easement is a land-use provision between real estate or other registered units or buildings. Since the main purpose here is to serve the use or management of land and water areas as opposed to serving the individual needs of the owner or possessor, easement is not classified as a security interest. Of course, it is guaranteed in the real estate register, but the creation and change of easements requires the participation of authorities (see paragraph 208 above).

Chapter 5. Joint Ownership

§1. Joint Ownership of Immovable Property

I. General Observations

238. Joint ownership is one category of property rights. A body of assets or an individual real estate can be jointly owned for different legal reasons (heritage, company, etc.). As a rule, joint owners have an equal share of property rights and joint decision-making concerning the property. This is true especially for transfer of the property or for using it as security for a loan or a claim. The Act on Joint Ownership (180/1958) provides detailed rules concerning the management of the property and also the dissolution of joint ownership. In the case of real estate or a parcel of it, one owner has the right, on certain conditions, to have his share separated in order to create an independent real estate unit of his own with the arrangement taking place in the form of a land survey. The same also applies to the distribution of all shares to the joint owners. If shares cannot, for different reasons, be separated, the court may decide that the joint ownership will be terminated by sale of the property at a public auction.

239. Heritage is a common category of joint ownership as is property that is in a company. A joint estate has to be settled before the individual items of property can be distributed to the holders of shares. Depending on the situation, the administration and settlement of a joint estate is a duty of the inheritors or by the court-appointed administrator. If necessary, a separate executor of the testamentary provisions may also be appointed. Within three months after the death, an inventory of the property must be made according to rules prescribed by law. After the settlement of the estate, the distribution to inheritors and beneficiaries may follow. The direct heirs are entitled to obtain a so-called legitim portion; in practice, this is half the value of the property. This right limits the part of the estate which would otherwise be given to beneficiaries. Moreover the right can only be set aside under specific circumstances. The surviving spouse, if married, inherits the estate if there are no direct heirs. According to the Marriage Act, spouses may have joint and private property. If not excluded by contract, a marital right brings a mutual expectancy to the other spouse's property in case of divorce or death. The spouse's residential property may thus be partly inheritable and partly belong to the surviving spouse privately or through the marital right. In order to avoid expulsion of the surviving spouse from their common home or real estate in the event of death of one spouse, the surviving spouse is entitled to possess the common holding or apartment undivided, even when there are direct heirs or beneficiaries.

240. The distribution of an estate to the heirs, involving either movable or immovable property, follows similar rules. The document on distribution or partition is equal to a deed of conveyance. Thus, a separate deed of conveyance is not required. The administrator of the distribution may be either chosen by the inheritors or appointed by the court. The material content of the distribution may also be agreed upon by the inheritors. The partition document is official when signed by the administrator or by all parties in the estate. The document is proof of ownership for the real estate register. The registration creates the individual rights of the heirs or other shareholders.

II. Co-ownership Applied to Apartment Buildings

A. Joint Ownership of Blocks and Flats

241. The Act on Habitation Right Flats (650/1990) creates a system of habitation in the legal area between lease and ownership. The system partly provides public financing for the construction of habitations; and partly establishes a protection position for the entitled person as possessor of his habitation.

242. A right to habitation is defined as the right of a private person to possess an apartment and eventually other space in a building which has been financed by the State in accordance with specific legislation on public interest support for loans. Such a building has the status of a habitation right building. The owner of this building concludes a habitation right contract with the addressee of the habitation right, under terms provided by law. The holder of the right agrees to pay a habitation right fee and, in addition, a regular payment for the use of the habitation. Other terms on fees or payments are void.

243. In order to guarantee proper functioning of the system, permitted owners of the building concerned are defined by law. These are usually companies, foundations, habitation right associations and other corporations of public law acting as shareholders in the organization of owners. The name of the building and its owner must include the expression 'habitation right' for identification of the legal status. Other corporations may not use that name for their activities.

244. The habitation right contract must be concluded in writing; oral agreements are not binding for the holder of the habitation right. The contract has to comprise defined relevant elements of the relationship between owner and rightholder, especially concerning the parties, the object of the rights, as well as the payments. The habitation right fee is normally determined and limited in relation to the legislation concerning the public financing aid of habitation right apartments, in this case, for example, the construction and financing costs for the owner of the building. The owner has to keep a separate account for the loans and habitation right fees.

245. The entitlement for obtaining a habitation right is also regulated by law. The municipality shall issue public notice, inviting private persons to apply for the habitation rights. The personal qualifications of applicants relate mainly to social and economic conditions. Those who satisfy these conditions have priority, but other persons may also obtain habitation rights. If necessary, a numerical order for the applicants may be introduced by the municipality. In that sense, the system is also available for people who could afford other habitations as well. However, the municipality must approve the suitability of the applicants. The habitation right is transferable from one spouse to another or by a will without application under certain conditions.

246. The residents are entitled to participate in the administration and decision-making of the building. They are also entitled to obtain all necessary information concerning the current situation of the building. If the owner is organized as an association, the rules concerning administration and membership are regulated separately, corresponding to the legislation on associations.[40] The Act on Habitation Rights provides rules for liability for maintenance of the habitations, for sanctions in case of breach of contract, and the revision of the payment for use.

247. The building, its owner and inhabitants as shareholders are bound by restrictions on the use and transfer until the payment of the public habitation loan and related obligations are met (sections 50b and 51). Once met, the property comes under regular rules of possession and administration of property habitations, which are usually under the Act on Habitation Share Companies.

B. Private Building Complexes

248. The most common habitation structure in cities is the habitation company. It is structurally similar to share companies but the legislation, the Act on Habitation Share Companies (809/1991), shows certain additional characteristics. Business buildings are often organized as Real Estate Share Companies to which the general Companies Act applies.

249. Habitation share companies are usually composed of private owners. The company may own the building lot as well, but often the ground is owned by the municipality. If the construction has been supported by public financing, the company may have to follow certain conditions imposed by the financing institutions or by the law regulating the public law. Occasionally, the State supports the construction of new housing areas by granting guarantees for loans or tax reductions. The shareholders themselves may also have to respect certain limitations of their power as long as the loan is not paid. The creation of a habitation company is not limited. A lot may be acquired on the commercial market or by leasing land from private or public investors. The land may also be acquired in the name of a company for the establishment. The landowner pays real estate tax to the municipality.

250. A habitation share company is defined as a company with the objective of owning and possessing one or more buildings where more than a half of the comprehensive floor area is assigned to be used by the shareholders as habitations. One or more of the shares are also assigned to possess one individual habitation or part of a building as defined in the by-laws of the company. The act is also applicable to other companies with the same objective but in which less than half of the shares

40. Act on Habitation Right Associations (1072/1994), Associations Act (503/1989).

are assigned to be used by the shareholders as habitations. However, in this case, the company may not use the name 'habitations share company'.

1. Commercial Trade with Habitation Shares under Construction

251. If shares for habitation are sold in buildings under planning or construction, the Act on Habitation Trade (843/1994) applies. The aim of the legislation is to give protection to the buyer in case the building project, for one reason or another, does not proceed as promised in the deed and attached plans. The establishing party has to arrange the adoption of security documents for the housing company and to file them as required by law. The establisher also has to deposit securities in order to ensure the fulfilment of eventual claims of the buyers and the company. If advance payment is required and paid, it will be used as part of the sale price. If the contract fails to be concluded for reasons attributable to the buyer, the seller may keep the paid amount.

2. Right to Exploitation in Shifts of Buildings for Use by Tourism

252. A rather common mode of organizing tourist activities is timeshare housing. There are a number of providers, and they offer timeshare objects both in Finland and abroad. Consumer legislation regulates trade with immovable properties on a timeshare basis (Consumer Protection Act, Chapter 10). The legislation is in line with the European Timeshare Directive (94/47/EC of the European Parliament and the Council of 26 October 1994 on the protection of purchasers in respect to certain aspects of contracts relating to the purchase of the right to use immovable properties on a timeshare basis). Presently (June 2007), the Commission has adopted a proposal for a new Directive which will enhance consumer protection by extending the scope of the current rules to also include the new products which have emerged in the market, such as holiday clubs. Resale and exchange will also be covered. The new rules should ensure that consumers are equally well protected throughout the EU and will create a level playing field in the market for timeshare and other holiday-related products.

253. The Finnish rules on consumer protection were adapted to EC law in 1997. The law comprises the consumer aspect specifically, whereas normal contract law applies in other respects, depending on the mode of habitation. The Consumer Act regulates marketing of timeshare habitations and timeshare objects (habitations including joint spaces and services). The parties concerned are the trader as seller and the client as buyer. Certain requirements set by the act in favour of the buyer are mandatory and exceptions made by contract are void. If the habitation is located within the European Economic Area (EEA), the Finnish legislation will apply in cases where the law of the location provides weaker protection to the client than Finnish law does. Professional traders must prepare a marketing document containing at least all necessary information foreseen by the Consumer Act (Chapter 10, section 4). This covers details about the seller or provider of the object, description of the timeshare conditions, including information about the law in the State of location, detailed presentation of the timeshare object, and available habitations as well as joint services. The document must also give information about prices and costs related to the object and the use of facilities, details concerning cancellation of the contract as well as the position of the object in an eventual resale system. For objects under construction, additional requirements of information are envisaged. Further provisions deal with consumer protection in terms of concluding and interpreting as well as dissolving the contract.

§2. Joint Ownership of Movable Property

254. The legislation on joint ownership applies to movable property as well. This means that a decision concerning transactions or use of the property requires an agreement or consent of all co-owners. They may agree contractually about the distribution of the possession of movable property, e.g., chattels in an estate. However, the holder of such a part needs the consent of the others to sell or lease it. The same also applies to mortgage or pledge of movable property.

Chapter 6. Neighbourhood and Urban Relations

255. Neighbourhood relations are regulated in a specific act (Neighbourhood Relations Act 26/1960). Originally, this act provided rules for the location of buildings, for agreements concerning qualifications of use, for the partitioning of border vegetation, and for the tolerance of nuisances. To a large extent, these civil law rules have been either abolished, or they have lost their relevance because most of the topics have been later on covered by public law, especially concerning buildings and industrial activities. When the act was prepared, the legislation on planning law did not exist and public building law was only available to some extent. However, neighbourhood law still has its function, e.g., in cases where a building license would violate the neighbour's rights, and his consent is therefore required. Parts of neighbourhood law have also been moved to water legislation, and some other environmental topics are incorporated in public environmental law.

256. Planning and building law provides for general rules on the location of buildings in relation to borderlines of building lots (LUBA, sections 116–117). In detailed areas, the plan often prescribes the exact location of buildings (LUBA, section 135). The distance must be estimated by the building permit authority to be 'sufficient' from buildings, public roads and neighbouring areas. In the Neighbourhood Relations Act, additional rules are enacted in respect of hazardous installations, especially buildings involving risk of fire or explosion as well as windmills (section 2: the distance must be at least 15 m from the borderline and 30 m from neighbouring buildings, gardens, and other exploited spots). The owner may, however, give his consent for deviations from these requirements. Such consent is not necessarily binding on permit authorities, for instance, if there is a risk of safety or health involved. The traditional priority rule is also applicable. This means that if the building or installations existed when the neighbourhood situation was initiated, the owner of the building or installation is protected against claims for removal. The consent is binding on successors as well without further administrative acts, although the owner of the building may have to give proof of the existence of consent. The consent also remains valid if the building or installation happens to be destroyed and is replaced by a new one or otherwise restored.

257. Additional rules concerning the location and use of animal shelters and individual sanitation arrangements protect the neighbouring property against harmful impacts. As far as vegetation on the borderline is concerned, the neighbour is entitled to remove roots invading his property, and also branches if the owner of the tree does not perform removal after being notified.

258. As far as digging and other works affecting the ground are concerned, the undertaker of the works must ensure that neighbouring buildings are not endangered. Damage must be compensated unless the reason for damage was lack or deficiency in the constructions of the building itself. The operator is also entitled to enter the neighbouring property in order to protect it against damage if it is necessary for protection or for minimizing costs. The neighbour may not prohibit it but he is entitled to receive compensation for damage caused by those measures. On the other hand, if there is a risk of a building or construction collapsing and causing damage to the neighbouring property, the owner of the building must be notified, and if he neglects to take measures, the neighbour may perform necessary works and obtain compensation from the other party. The same applies to the relationship of possessors of concerned real estate and parcels. According to public law, constructions affecting the ground level or the natural flow of water may require a terrain construction permit unless the change is foreseen in a detailed plan (LUBA, section 128).

259. The prohibition of abuse of owner's or possessor's rights (chicane) is also adopted in the Neighbourhood Relations Act (section 13). The measure may as such be legally permitted, but if the main intention is to cause damage or harm to the neighbour, the damaged party has the right to claim for compensation and restoration of the land. The claim must be presented during the year after the event or the appearance of damage. This academically interesting ruling has limited practical relevance nowadays. However, neighbours may suffer from the use of buildings and other constructions, especially in recreation areas, which have been erected too close to each other or which, according to applicable regulations, did not require a building permit. Noise caused by living activities is, however, difficult to allocate under the prohibition mentioned above; instead, administrative regulations (health) are applicable to fix the appropriate level of admissible noise.

260. Neighbourhood relations which are not agreed upon or are to some extent not in conformity with legal or administrative regulations as stipulated to protect the neighbour, are in principle not protected against later claims of the neighbour. He may demand removal or correction of a construction to which he has not consented. However, if he does not react 'immediately', the construction may remain as it is, unless it was erected intentionally or negligently against valid prescriptions, for instance, planning provisions. The neighbour who loses his right of action is entitled to compensation if the defect causes him damage or inconvenience; the negligently erected building may for instance have negative effect on his own building rights. If the compensation is prescribed annually, the real estate is under a lien for the amount and its interest. The lien will be entered in the property register as well.

261. If the borderline between parcels on forest land is not marked in loco, the owners are entitled to mark the line and for that purpose to remove the vegetation, usually up to 1.5 m. Felled trees belong to the estate where they grew. The measure usually is based on consent, but it may also be undertaken against the will of the other party who then pays the costs as well.

262. Neighbours are under obligation to permit mutually the placement of cables, pipes and conduits and to erect necessary constructions on the land of neighbouring real estate. This right applies to equipment which is required for the domestic use of the real estate or parcel as well as leased land. A balance of interests is foreseen. According to public law, an owner of land may apply for an authority's permit (easement) to place installations on land and water areas. This right is not limited to domestic use but may also apply, for instance, to municipal water, telephone and sanitation companies. In all cases, the owner of the burdened area is entitled to compensation.

263. Today, the most important provision in the Neighbourhood Relations Act appears to be the prohibition against causing unreasonable nuisance (section 17). According to this provision, land, a building or an apartment may not be used to the extent that its use causes an unreasonable burden to the neighbour from environmentally harmful substances as well as dust, smoke, smell, vibration, light, heat, and more. In estimating reasonableness, local conditions are taken into account. Also, if the detrimental factor existed before the neighbour relationship occurred, the priority rule may protect the operator against claims from the neighbour. If the neighbour claims removal or cessation of the activity, the suit should be brought within three years. For compensation, other time limits apply.

264. The role of the provision is today rather limited since the Environmental Pollution Act (86/2000) regulates the need for a permit and the setting of limits for causing environmental pollution or health risks. The Environmental Damages Act (737/1994) again provides for compensation rules in case on environmental pollution on the basis of strict liability. For this reason, the prohibition against causing an unreasonable burden applies mainly to direct injury or impact on someone's property, rather than harm caused by environmental impacts. Causing a health risk is forbidden and unreasonable in all situations.

265. Construction of private roads to satisfy the need for access to real estate through other areas is regulated in the Private Roads Act (358/1962). This Act relates to the system of survey legislation (Real Estate Formation Act 1995). The 'private road right' is a category of easement with three main subcategories, namely (1) the right to build a new private road (basic private road right), (2) the right to obtain access to an existing road, and (3) the right to build or use a road for specific transportations, especially forest traffic.

Part II. Movable Property and Personal Property

Chapter 1. General Classification

266. Movable property is composed of specific goods and fungibles. Fungibles are identified by quality and quantity. Specific goods are defined as individual objects having specific characteristics. The relevance of this distinction is apparent, for instance, in a sale. In case of fungibles, the buyer does not acquire the property before the identification thereof through separation. Also, the subject of a pledge must be identified before the act is valid. It is possible to identify fungibles by determining the location and nature of the subject, e.g., a store or a part of it. Such an entity or chattel may also serve as security for a movable mortgage if it is registered (Business Chattel Registration Act). In consumer law (Act 416/1994), the terms 'merchandise' or 'product' are used as corresponding expressions.

267. Vessels are specific objects. Vessels in commercial traffic must be registered. Also civil vessels exceeding a certain size must be registered. Registered vessels are suitable for mortgaging. They cannot be used for pledge. Similar rules apply to aircraft and cars.

268. Buildings are either immovable or movable property depending on the relationship to the ground. If the owner is the same, buildings are constituent parts of the immovable property; if the building belongs, for instance, to a tenant, the building is classified as movable property. Movable property may be rented under the House Rent Act (481/1995).

§1. Tangible Movable Property in Possession

269. The concept of movable property or 'a thing' has relevance in different areas of the legislation. It may appear as an object under lost property law, antiquities legislation, security regulations, and more. Also extracted natural resources (wood, minerals and stone) are movable property. Possession of tangible objects indicates ownership with some exceptions. The possessor may transfer the title by handing the property over to the receiver. Money in this sense may be movable property, especially in the case of foreign currency as opposed to local currency. The main categories of bonds are promissory notes and order bonds. The distinction is that promissory notes are closely dependant on the underlying obligation between creditor and debtor, whereas order bonds are transferable and bound to the document (see Promissory Notes Act 622/1947).

270. Bond securities are movable property. Their legal position depends on the category of the documents. There is no general definition of bond securities. In literature, it is defined as a document, the possession of which is a necessary precondition for the use of the right vested in the document. The debtor may effectively discharge his obligation solely to the holder of the document or having proof of its possession. The document, therefore, represents the title, and original relationship between the creditor and debtor is irrelevant. The original creditor cannot claim performance from the debtor after fulfilment of the obligation to the possessor of the document. Negotiable securities are defined as bond securities which have the quality of guaranteeing the possessor protection against claims from third parties, e.g., previous holders of the document. Categories of bond securities are bearer papers or order bonds, bills of exchange, and cheques. The corresponding legislation will not be presented here.

§2. Intangible Movable Property in Action

I. Concept

271. Intangible movable property is defined as a right which is not physical, (i.e., perceptible to the senses) but rather an incorporeal value or interest. Such a thing is usually bound to a document or registration which identifies the content and the holder of the right. The legal order usually presupposes the use of action against eventual violators of those rights because the violation could not be physically observed, for instance in taking possession thereof. Transfer of intangible rights may require specific conditions concerning the assignee, partly in order to give him legal protection against third parties, but in some cases also to ensure that he has the required expertise to control the use of the right, in order to avoid social or economic damage.

272. Promissory notes, which are not freely endorseable by giving possession, refer to this category; the document entitles the creditor to raise action against the debtor concerning a specific deal. Other promissory notes, which are negotiable by endorsement, fall under the rules of tangible movable property, since possession of the document is in itself a satisfactory requirement for raising action. The sanctions which are available in case of breach against intangible rights are usually action for a prohibition or compensation.

II. Patent and Other Intangible Rights

273. Patents are an important category of intangible rights (Patents Act 550/ 1967). The regulations have been adapted to the requirements of the European Community (European Patent Convention 1973) and international conventions. A patent gives the holder an exclusive right to decide upon the use and transfer of the subject of an invention. The national patent agency has the competence to decide in matters concerning approval and registration of patents. In addition, international patents can be applied for in another State as well, in accordance with the international convention on patent cooperation. Specific rules apply to patents on biotechnological inventions, in order to limit the use of patent protection on natural organic processes or on ethically questionable experiments on human beings. Otherwise, the conditions concerning approval of a patent follow the traditional scheme: the invention must be new and differ from what was known when the application was made to the authority. Artistic and technical works as such are not patentable.

274. The patent prevents others from making use of the invention in any economically profitable way without the consent of the holder of the patent. In case of biological material, the patent protects most technical or biological modes of the development of that material. Also a technical process may be patented if it is essentially depending on the characteristics of the biological material in question.

275. Patent rights may be granted to applicants domiciled in a State of the European Community other than Finland. Such an applicant must have a representative in Finland for administrative purposes. The holder of a patent may grant a license to use the patent. The assignee may only transfer the license to a third party with the consent of the owner of the patent. A compulsory license may be granted by a court after three years validity of the patent in cases where the patent has not been used or essentially developed in Finland. There are specific provisions concerning the compulsory licensing of inventions on plant breeding. The use of plant materials may be vital for professional farming or research. Therefore, a cultivator may apply for a license, without exclusivity, to make use of the patent to the extent it is required for the plants he is cultivating.

276. On the other hand, the cultivator may also have an intangible right to his method of breeding in accordance with the Act on Plant Breeding Rights (789/ 1992). The holder of the patent may apply for a compulsory right to use the breeding right if it is required for the profitable use of the patent in question. A patent is valid for twenty years. Disputes concerning rights to patent and licenses are within the competence of the court. Appeal against an administrative decision on an application goes to the Supreme Administrative Court.

277. The Plant Breeding Act has transposed the harmonized European system and the requirements of the convention of the International Union for the Protection of New Varieties of Plants (UPOV). The conditions for approval of the right, the registration and the content of the right are internationally harmonized. The Patent Act also provides rules concerning granting European patent and the procedure of application there for. Such a patent may be granted according to the European Patent Convention by the European Patent Office.

278. There are other intangible rights with a comparable system of priority and protection. A utility model or patent may be granted on the basis of a (to some extent) lower requirement of patentability than a patent (Act on Utility Models 800/1991). There are also other mechanisms for granting exclusivity to producers or developers, for instance in the technical area, especially the legal protection of topographies of semiconductor products as stipulated in the Council Directive 87/54/EEC, which has been correspondingly transposed into Finnish law (Act 32/1991).

279. Further pieces of legislation in relation to immaterial rights are the Copyright Act (404/1961) and the Trade Mark Act (7/1964).

§3. Funds

280. Relevant acts concerning funds are the Securities Market Act (495/1989) which regulates the activity of stock companies, the Act on Investment Funds (48/1999), the Act on Real Estate Funds (1173/1997), the Act on Stock Traders (579/1996), the Act on Foreign Investors' Right to Services in Finland (580/1996), the Act on Book-entry System (826/1991, the Act on Book-entry Accounts (827/1991). The market is open for all clients, and bond securities and other commercial papers are usually transferable according to general rules on endorsement and mortgaging.

Chapter 2. Legal Interests

§1. Movable Property

I. General

281. Movable or personal property can be defined in a negative way as non-immovable property. In real estate law, movable property may be either related to land or connected to a person as a holder of a limited right. In other words, in some situations, movable property is attached to immovable and follows its legal destiny. If, for instance, an industrial installation is composed of land, machineries, and equipment; a mortgage may cover the movable parts of the installation, which as a consequence means that these cannot be separated from the industrial unit, at least not without the consent of the mortgagees. In case of transfer of real estate, movable property may or may not remain with the buyer, depending on the contract. Otherwise, as a rule, the seller is entitled to remove those parts of the property which are not immovable elements of the object. In case of land lease, buildings that are erected by the tenant are usually his property and hence movable property; otherwise, the buildings are constituent parts of the real estate and consequently immovable property. The same is true in the relationship between a building and its constituent parts: parts of the building are not separate objects and they therefore follow the ownership of the building.

282. For tangible objects, it is usually typical that they can be separated and moved without physical changes. In cases that involve land resources (stones, vegetation, etc.), this feature does not usually apply. In Finnish law, however, the distinction lies more on the legal plane rather than at a physical or material level. If a separation from the immovable context is allowed or contractually agreed upon, the object or the right to that object is defined as immovable. Some legislation, such as the rules on pledges, applies to tangible property only. Movable property is defined as the (limited) rights to movable objects in the same way as immovable property means ownership[41] of immovable objects.

II. Classification

283. Tangible objects are classified as fungibles and specific goods. The difference is mainly in the structure and utilization of the objects. For fungibles, it is typical that the object is not defined or materialized before its separation. If a contract is aimed towards a sale of cloth, flour or similar mass products, the buyer cannot claim the object before it has been taken apart. The seller may, depending on the contract, choose which source he uses for the separation. This also has the effect that the buyer is not the owner before the separation. This equally applies to pledges and mortgages of movable property. If again a specific object is sold, the contract

41. As well as certain (rare) permanent rights to possession of land, see Kartio, 69.

transfers – usually connected to transfer of possession – the title of ownership. The difference between the two categories of movable objects is not always clear or decisive within the legal evaluation. Fungibles may be defined in detail (cloth from a defined roll, flour from a specific container, an appointed book in the bookstore, etc.) which limits the need or possibility of separation.

284. Certain categories of objects are regulated separately from movable property in general and, therefore, it is not necessary to classify them in more precise terms. Examples of these objects are vessels, buildings, motor vehicles, bonds and money. In particular, a vessel may be defined as a means of transportation used for navigation. The term does not include rowboats or other vehicles with a limited steering capability. The specific regulation on registration of vessels covers vehicles in merchant shipping and other vehicles filling certain technical criteria. Similar rules also exist for aircrafts and motor vehicles.

285. It was already mentioned earlier that buildings erected by a tenant are his property and hence movable property; otherwise the buildings are constituent parts of the real estate. However, there are some differences depending on the category of land lease. The strongest title one may grant is the lease of a building lot (a ground rent): here all the buildings emanate with the lease into the ownership of the tenant. The reason for this is that during the relatively long-lasting lease period, the tenant disposes of the building right. Buildings as movable property are, however, in some cases treated in the same manner as immovable property for practical reasons, for instance, in mortgage and marriage law. Buildings without ownership of land may also be subject to expropriation.

286. Bond securities are physical in the sense that the document constitutes proof of a debt or other commitment determined in the document. A bond security is defined as a document of civil law for which possession is a necessary requirement. There are several categories of bond securities, some of them entitling the possessor to receive a certain amount of money (promissory note, cheque, bill of exchange, life insurance policy), a specific object (bill of lading, deposit receipt), or a right in a share (share certificate). Stock certificates have been replaced by a registration system which abolishes the need for individual documents to prove the title.

287. Money may be treated as a tangible object, especially foreign currency and money that is not in circulation. In these cases, the rules on protection of ownership (e.g., owner's right to redeem the object from a not entitled possessor) apply. When dealing with current money as means of payment, the situation falls under the general rules of bond securities, the effect of which is that possession is decisive as proof of ownership.

288. Trade in movable property is regulated under the Act of Commerce (355/1987), and the regulations cover change of movable property as well. According to the general classification of movable objects, property includes a building, immovable installation or construction on the land of another owner. This act does not apply to these in cases where usufruct to the land has been established; these situations are ruled by the law on lease and tenancy. Freedom of contract as well as trade custom and practice allow deviations from the rules of the act. However, these rules are binding if the contract or custom would be unreasonable for one of the parties. The act does not apply to consumer protection (see Consumer Act 38/1978). The Commerce Act provides for rules concerning misrepresentation, the ultimate sanction being dissolution of the sale.

289. The Commercial Code of the General Law of 1734 (CC) is still a valid law to the extent that it regulates legality of a contract in cases where a third party claims against the sale. The extinction rule for sale to two successive buyers is that the first buyer may keep the object (CC Chapter 1, section 5).

290. The law on obligations (Contracts Act 228/1929) provides a general background for agreements on property law regulated in specific laws. The Contracts Act also provides rules that are especially used for the conclusion of a valid contract ('offer and reply', sections 1–8),[42] for the modification of contracts on the basis of invalidity and the unreasonableness as well as the use of authority.[43] The powers of a trustee and guardian are regulated separately (see paragraph 508). Conveyance of immovable property requires authority in writing. In particular, the authority must be signed by the seller, identify the agent, and specify the object under contract. Open authority is not sufficient, and the attesting notary must verify the agent (REC, Chapter 2, section 3).

291. There are different degrees of contractual defects or deficiencies, partly depending on whether the addressee was in good faith or not. According to the Contract Act (sections 28–38) a contract is invalid in following situations:

- use of essential force involving violence or threat;
- fraud or deceitful seduction;
- misuse of a party's poor financial trouble, comprehension, or irresponsibility in a manner that the other party gained disproportionate profit;
- textual misrepresentation if the addressee was in bad faith;
- error caused by technical transmission;[44]
- contract was concluded under dishonourable or immoral conditions of which the party was aware;
- false document on debt or right in case that the addressee was not in good faith.

292. If a bearer bond signed by the debtor is unintentionally transferred to a third party, the receiver may invoke the document if he was labouring under the notion

42. Provisions on acceptance of offers in an auction are provided in s. 9 of the Act. The highest offer stays till the immediate next higher offer.
43. Individual authority based on notice or letter of attorney, authorization based on position and proxy. Exaggeration of the power is not binding for the assigner if the addressee knew or should have known of this excess.
44. The sender has to notify the addressee about the error; otherwise the message is binding as it was received if the receiver was in good faith.

of good faith. The possession of a bearer bond is thus similar to possession of tangible objects where possession implies ownership. If someone lent money against a receipt which the creditor loses, the debtor may pay his debt with legal effect to the presenter of the receipt. This payment is binding against the creditor if the debtor acted in good faith (section 35).

III. Mediation of Terms

293. A contract term may be unreasonable or later appear to lead to unreasonable consequences. Such a term may be modified or set aside. In evaluating what is unreasonable, the whole contractual situation may be taken into consideration, not just a selected part of it (section 36). Whether or not such a modification would cause destruction of the whole contract, the content can be mediated or dissolved also as to parts other than its unreasonable parts.[45] A clause according to which a pledge or other security would be lost if the contract is not fulfilled is not enforceable. A contract which would limit a party's right to carry on in a competing profession is not binding if it would limit his professional liberty to an unreasonable extent.

§2. Movable Limited Real Rights

294. Limited rights may be established in a property or its parts, constituents, or appurtenances. These parts are normally thought to serve the real estate and be attached to the property and, hence, belong to the property of the owner. Limited rights established in these parts need to be formally recognized and registered. A lease of a real property or its part does not require registration because the tenant's possession is a satisfactory proof of his real right.

I. Guaranteed Real Rights in Movables

A. *Loan*

295. Movable objects may be subject to loan and all varieties of objects are suitable for loan. The same rules apply to tangible objects and living objects, creatures, and plants (Commercial Code, Chapter 11). In cases that involve lending, this means that the owner gives possession without receiving compensation; however, some general rules apply. First, the borrower must take care of the object and return it in the same condition it was at the beginning. If the object requires maintenance, it must not be allowed to deteriorate. The borrower may not use the object as a pledge for his own or other person's obligations unless the owner has consented to the pledge or to keeping the object as security for invested costs.

45. In case of consumer law, specific rules on mediation apply (Consumer Act 38/1978).

296. Different types of transactions concerning the loaned object are forbidden to the borrower. The borrower may not, without the consent of the owner or his assignee, sell, pledge, or give away any loaned property. If this happens, the owner has the right to redeem the property. If the receiver acted in bad faith, he must return the object to the owner without compensation.

B. Movable Leases

1. In General

297. Movable property under lease covers two main categories: (1) lease of tangible objects, such as vehicles, machines and installation products and (2) lease of habitations and business facilities. Tenancy of a house without lease of the real estate (land) is regulated under movable property (see paragraph 175).

298. If a movable object has been leased twice, the priority rule applies, and the first contractor may keep the object.[46] There is also, in general, a prohibition against leasing property without the consent of the owner. Should someone rent property that is not his own, he is liable to pay the rent to the owner, and he may also be subject to a fine.

299. A lease contract is binding in most cases without further formal requirements, on the terms agreed upon in the lease contract. If an advance payment has not been agreed, it cannot be claimed afterwards.

2. Leasing

300. Leasing is used as an instrument for enabling the leasing holder to possess and manage both movable and immovable property. The object is designed to have a sufficient lifetime and a value to cover the costs of the financing and administration. An institution or concept was established in Finland in the 1960s, which in its beginning was solely used for leasing of movable property. There are two categories of leasing, namely financial leasing and operating leasing. Both types are aimed at the creation of a legally protected position for the leasing holder to use a piece of property. Financial leasing comprises two transactions, purchase and lease which are combined to a financial arrangement. The financing lessor buys from the seller an object which the leaseholder will use in his business and which he receives from the lessor by leasing. The leaseholder typically indentifies the object and the provider in advance before the financial arrangement. The financing lessor usually does not act as an expert concerning the qualities of the object and therefore also is not responsible for defects in the object. Depending on the conditions of the financial

46. Commercial Code 1734, Ch. 14, s. 2. The content of the contract with the second tenant lacks relevance.

lease agreement, the leaseholder may directly make the provider responsible for such defaults in the delivery.[47]

As far as movables, e.g., machinery and vehicles, are concerned, leasing is a financial tool which eventually implies the right of the leasing holder to redeem the property at the end. This system was introduced by financing companies and it lacks specific legislation. Leasing is used mostly in trade between firms.

301. Leasing of real property is a category of financial leasing with real estate as the subject. The financing arrangement based on 'sale and leaseback' means that a firm sells its own real estate to a financing company. At the same time the financing company leases the real estate to the seller (lease holder). The possession and utilization remain through the whole procedure in the hands of the lease holder. The contract may include the option or right of the lease holder to redeem the property under specific conditions. Since the lease holder is the original owner, the financing company as the lessor is not liable for eventual deficiencies or risks inherent in the property. The leasing of real property may be used as a part of larger corporate arrangements as well. The object serves as security in the hands of the lessor. The rules providing protection of the leasing holder as tenant against creditors of the lessor are not always clear but are usually adopted from general law on security and tenancy.

47. See the Decision of the Supreme Court KKO:2008:53/23.5.2008: the financial lessor was made responsible for defects in the object.

Chapter 3. Publicity of Movable Real Rights

§1. Role of Possession

302. Possession is important when defining ownership of tangible property, since possession implies ownership. In addition to the common situation where the possessor has an object under lease, there are certain other situations where one may hold in his possession movable objects which are not his property. Two main categories are loan of movable property and deposit of tangible objects.

§2. Registration of Movable Goods

303. Certain categories of movable property are registered in order to provide legal information concerning ownership, possession, mortgage, leasing and others. Registration also serves the control of technical security in instances that include movable machines, especially vehicles.

I. Business Chattels Mortgage

304. According to the Business Chattels Mortgage Act (634/1984), movable property may be registered as an object of mortgage. A merchant who is registered in the trade register may mortgage his registered movable property as security without transferring possession, in accordance with the provisions of the Act. Security may be given for a bill drawn in favour of bearer or a named person as well as by the person appointed as receiver to cover the capital, as well as interest and collection costs (promissory note secured by pledge). The National Board of Patents and Registration of Trademarks is the competent registering authority which also keeps the business mortgage register.[48]

305. Movable property that is suitable for pledge is described and listed in the Act (section 3). The property may include four main categories of objects and values:

(1) physical property items, such as buildings, machineries, chattels and comparable materials;
(2) tangible rights and limited rights, including leased property;
(3) raw materials, substances, and current assets; and
(4) cash flow, bond securities, and other financial instruments.

A joint mortgage cannot be granted for the same obligation on the business property of two or more merchants.

48. Appeal against the authority's decision may be raised at the Court of Appeal of Helsinki.

II. Vessel as Security

306. The mortgage of a vessel as security is regulated under the Vessel Mortgage Act (211/1927). A vessel which has been entered in the vessel register may be given as security for a monetary obligation. The security requires the consent of the owner of the vessel, and the mortgage is effective as soon as it has been entered in the register. Several vessels may serve as security for one obligation only if they belong to the same owner. A registered or registrable vessel may not be given in possession as a pledge. Vessels under construction may be registered in the vessel construction register and used as security. Mortgaging can be applied for by either the owner of the vessel or the creditor.

307. Certain vehicles may be used as security for monetary obligations in accordance with the Vehicle Mortgage Act (810/1972). The formal requirement here is that the vehicle be registered according to law,[49] and that the obligation be based on a written document. Regular passenger cars may not be used as security; objects available for mortgage are trucks, buses, and certain specialist or professional vehicles and machinery. Only one vehicle may be used as security for an obligation at the same time. Transfer of possession as pledge is not possible for registered vehicles. The security is effective when the owner has given his consent, and the competent authority has registered the transaction. A mortgage gives priority in respect of the vehicle, its accessories as well as insurance indemnity. The validity period of the mortgage is ten years, but in order to keep the security in force, the mortgage must be renewed. The owner who holds the deed of obligation may reuse the mortgage for another obligation with the original priority. If the value of the vehicle decreases unexpectedly, immediate fulfilment of the obligation may be claimed before maturity. A vehicle remains in the register as long as the mortgage is in force.

308. Aircraft, if registered or registrable, may likewise be used as security and mortgaged according to the Aircraft Mortgage Act (211/1928). The competent authority is the Central Aviation Administration.[50]

III. Registration of Usufruct and Limited Rights

A. *General Remarks*

309. The law does not prescribe or set restrictions against providing limited rights by contract or other disposition. In certain categories, there is a need to provide legal protection for the possession of the weaker party. Accordingly, the regulations on land tenancy and rent of habitation may envisage either procedural requirements or deny the validity of terms which are not in conformity with law.

49. Competent authority is the Central Motor-Vehicle Administration.
50. Aviation Act 1242/2005.

The protection is directed either against the party (landlord) in order to prevent illegal annulment of the contract or against the successor of the landlord who might refuse to recognize the existence of the contract (Habitation Rent Act 481/1995 and Land Tenancy Act 258/1966). In order to guarantee the validity of limited rights, especially in the latter category, a limited right may or must be registered in the property register, depending on the category of the limited right. Without registration, contractual rights may not be enforceable against successors of the other party. This means that those rights, if not registered, are binding between the parties only and bona fide third parties, with some exceptions. It is important to note that limited rights (i.e., easements), which have been established in a procedure (survey) and are aimed at a mostly permanent usufruct between real estate parcels cannot be registered in the property register because their validity is guaranteed differently: these land-use prescriptions are marked under the title of each parcel of real estate concerned in the land register.

B. Registrable Limited Rights

310. All limited rights cannot be registered. A limited right may have its legal basis in a bilateral contract, but other acts of private law may also establish a limited right in favour of someone else (donation, will, or a life-annuity disposition). The conditions for registration do not depend on the character of the act but on the limited right itself and its content. However, not every special or limited right is acceptable for registration. The list of limited rights capable of registration consists of the most common and established categories of limited rights (REC, Chapter 14 section 1). The categories of registrable rights are:

(1) a lease or other usufruct;
(2) a right to derive a pension from real estate;
(3) a right to take timber; and
(4) a right to excavate land or mineral resources or another comparable right of extraction.

311. To maintain clarity of the registration system, registered rights must fit into those categories.[51] Other rights are, of course, valid between parties in accordance with general contractual rules, but lack of registration may have consequences for the legal status of the right. The categories of limited rights listed above have their bases in the corresponding specified legislation (see paragraph 123).

51. In specified legislation, registration of rights may be prescribed; these provisions overrule those of the Real Estate Code. For instance a contractual right to receive permanent usufruct of water power is registrable (Water Act, Ch. 8, s. 3).

C. *Registrability*

312. Only rights established between persons – not between real estate and other registered units – can be registered. For this reason, permanent rights cannot be registered. This is partly due to the substantial legislation on contractual rights where rights are only allowed for a limited time. Permanent rights are usually established to serve real estate as an easement or comparable specific right.[52] A contractual right to take timber may be concluded between parties on a general contractual basis but, to protect its duration, the right may be registered for a maximum period of five years. On the other hand, an excavation right (soil resources, etc.) may be registered for up to fifty years from the establishment of the right. As far as usufruct is concerned, statute law may set different time limits. These are consequently also the time limits for which they may be registered. No limited rights can be registered without a limitation on the period. If a new contract or disposition is entered, the time limit begins anew.

D. *Obligation and Right to Register*

313. If a limited right is intended to be transferable, registration of the right is required. The holder of a lease or another usufruct related to a real estate must apply for the registration of his right, if the usufruct is to be transferable to a third party without reference to the titleholder (REC, Chapter 14 section 2). Registration is also required if there are buildings or other constructions belonging to the usufructuary on the real estate, or it has been agreed that they may be built. This registration is intended to identify buildings and constructions belonging to the holder of the limited right; otherwise they would be viewed as consistent parts of the real estate and belong to the landlord. The obligation to apply for registration starts when the limited right has been established, or the holder of the right has possession on another contractual ground of acquisition. Usufruct may, for instance, have its basis as a term of a contract of sale in favour of the seller who receives a limited title of use.

314. Under the provisions on taxation of conveyance deeds, establishment of limited rights is submitted to taxation in the same way as conveyance of title of ownership. For this reason, registration should be applied for and the tax paid within a period of six months under a threat of a fine.[53]

IV. Joint Possession Agreement

315. If a real estate or another register unit is jointly owned and in equal shares, the shareholders may, instead of applying for a formal partition of the land property, enter a joint possession agreement. This document determines which physical parts of the property are possessed by each shareholder. In order to guarantee such

52. For the time periods of different categories of limited rights see Wirilander, 533–538.
53. Property Conveyance Tax Act, s. 5, REC Ch. 11, s. 6.

an agreement and the right to possess the shares agreed upon, the agreement may be registered (REC, Chapter 14, section 3). The benefit of such an agreement is that real estate, which for technical or economical reasons could not be partitioned, may still be profitably used individually by the holders of the shares.

V. Registration of Rights Relating to Buildings or Constructions

316. As mentioned above, a right belonging to someone other than the landowner in relation to a building, construction, machine, or facility used in business and contributing to the purpose or use of the real estate, may be registered (REC section 4). At this point there are certain conditions, namely that:

(1) the object has been built or brought on the real estate subject to a reservation or repossession clause or on the basis of a lease contract or another comparable agreement; or
(2) the object has been transferred to the usufructuary of the real estate as a part of the usufruct.

A right subject to a reservation of ownership or repossession clause may be registered to be in force for a maximum of five years from the conclusion of the agreement.

VI. Registration of Trade Components

317. In order to identify chattels for eventual separate use, it is possible to register components and accessories of real estate belonging to a trade carried out on it. This registration separates the components and accessories from the rest of the property (REC, Chapter 14, section 5). Such property may also be used for security (see paragraph 578). A declaration of the titleholder may be registered to the effect that the building or facility (identified in the declaration or otherwise defined as to its characteristics) used in business, owned, or later obtained by him, and permanently located on the real estate, either:

(1) does not belong to the real estate, even if it otherwise would be deemed a component or an accessory; or
(2) belongs to the real estate, even if it otherwise would not be deemed a component or an accessory.

318. The registration of limited rights may have as object (section 6):

(1) a real estate or a common entered into the land register;
(2) a parcel, the title to which has been registered; or
(3) a registered lease or usufruct.

VII. Legal Effects of Registration of Special or Limited Rights

319. The registration of a special right has similar legal effects to those provided for registration of title (REC, Chapter 13). If several registrable special rights have been attached to a real estate and they cannot be simultaneously fulfilled, then, as a rule, the right first attached prevails.

320. As far as precedence of the registered rights is concerned, the legal effects of registration of a special right begin on the day when the registration application has become pending. A registration earlier applied for on an earlier date takes precedence in relation to a registration or mortgage later applied for on a later date. A special right also takes precedence over a lien, based on a mortgage, applied for on the same day. In the event of rights which by nature exclude the enforcement of other rights, only the precedent right may be registered (e.g., a contract between joint owners concerning partition of the joint property).

321. For the registration procedure, similar rules apply as those which apply to registration of title (see paragraph 400). Application for registration may be made by the holder of the registrable right and by the titleholder of the real estate, and the application must include the contract or other document relating to the attachment or transfer of the registrable right. In certain situations, the consent of the titleholder is a prerequisite for registration. Moreover, the consent of all lienholders over the real estate may be a prerequisite to the registration. The same applies to a change in the order of precedence. If the property of the titleholder is under a business mortgage, the registration may, in certain situations, be made only if all the holders of the business mortgage consent to the same. Depending on the situation, the application may, if not approved, be left in abeyance or rejected on grounds defined by law.

322. Registration will be deleted after expiration of the term of validity of the right or on the basis of unexpected circumstances. However, an existing lien affects or defers the deletion of registration. The registration of a special right may not be deleted, even if it has lapsed before the full term due to termination, agreement, or another reason, before the mortgages and registrations of special rights to it have been cancelled. If the special right is subject to mortgages, the application for the deletion of the registration may be left in abeyance and notified to the lienholder. In the decision, the lien holder shall be called upon to bring an action for collection of the debt within three months of the notification. If the creditor fails to seek payment from the real estate within the set time limit and notify the same to the registering authority, the mortgage shall be cancelled and the registration of the special right may be deleted.

Part III. Acquisition of Property Rights

Chapter 1. Transfer of Property by Contract

§1. CONVEYANCE OF IMMOVABLE PROPERTY *INTER VIVOS*

I. Introduction

323. Acquisition of real estate by voluntary deed is regulated in the Real Estate Code (Part I, Chapters 1–5). The present legislation entered into force in the beginning of 1997. The Code applies to acquisition of real property by sale, trade, gift or other conveyance of real estate and other immovable property. If the acquisition is based on inheritance, will, distribution of matrimonial assets, expropriation, or anything other than conveyance, other rules apply. The provisions on the conveyance of real estate also apply to the conveyance of a share and a parcel of real estate, a common, a parcel, and a share of a common. Acquisition by heritage and will is regulated in the Heritage Code (HerC). Acquisition by expropriation and other compulsory measures of authorities is mainly under the Real Estate Expropriation Act (603/1977). Expropriation is available for public needs, in particular for the enforcement of zoning purposes, for road constructions, and for the creation of nature and cultural preserves.

II. Specific Characteristics

324. Sale by contract is the main category of voluntary conveyance of a title (REC, Chapter 2). A form of deed for sale must fulfil formal requirements. Thus, a sale of real estate must be concluded in writing. The seller and the buyer or their attorneys must sign the deed of sale. In addition, a notary must attest the sale in writing in the presence of all the signatories of the deed of sale (public attest). A deed has to also contain information stipulated by law.

Thus a deed of sale must indicate:

325. (1) true intent to convey;

The expression 'simulated transaction' implies that the parties have no real intent to transfer property rights. Such a contract is not valid even if the conveyance has been completed according to formal requirements.[54] However, if the buyer later concluded a contract with a third party to establish a limited right, such a contract is binding on the seller if the contracting party was in good faith about the buyer's title. Also, if ownership has been further transferred, the latest possessor may invoke his right in accordance with general rules in the Contract Act: if a simulated document has been drawn up and the holder under the document of a claim or a right has assigned the said right to a third party, the assignee is entitled to enforce the right if he acted in good faith at the time of acquisition (section 34).[55]

Assignment as security aims at giving protection to the creditor for a payment and hence implies that the creditor is the owner of the title as long as the debt exists. This category of interim ownership is not recognized by law and is not valid *inter partes*.[56]

326. (2) identification of the real estate to be conveyed;

The object must be identified and specified in the contract. This applies especially to parcels or lots which are not (yet) registered units and which cannot, therefore, be identified by the register. Map information is therefore recommended. However, there are situations where even a specified object may be subsequently interpreted in a divergent manner. For instance, in a survey procedure, the boundaries or natural features of the identified parcel may appear to be somewhat different from what has been documented. The survey commission may perform corrections and even deviate from the agreement if the parties agree. An essential deviation requires an additional contract of conveyance.

327. (3) definition of the seller and the buyer;

Identification of the parties to a contract is important because in certain situations the competence to conclude a contract may be restricted due to the need for consent or a permit and in situations of joint ownership (see paragraph 372 below).

328. (4) setting of the price or other consideration.

A sale is not binding unless it is concluded as provided in the Real Estate Code. This applies to any title to real estate which is acquired by sale, trade, gift or other conveyance. The regulatory requirement covers both the price as well as oral agreements which on this point are not legally valid. If the seller and the buyer have agreed on a price or other consideration in excess of that stated in the deed of sale, the seller is not entitled to collect the excess amount, agreed upon orally. However, some separate provisions apply to the acquisition of real estate by inheritance, will, distribution of matrimonial assets, expropriation or other transfer of ownership which are not performed by contractual conveyance. Before the entry into force of

54. Jokela, Kartio & Ojanen, 38 et seq. and Zitting & Rautiala, 291. The simulated deed is not binding valid *inter partes*, but its dissolution is automatic if the transfer has been registered or the property transferred to a third party. For the court's practice, see Zitting-Rautiala, 293 et seq.
55. Simulation or lack of real intent to convey is possible also by wrongly using the term 'transfer' for purposes of security or lease.
56. The decision of the Supreme Court KKO 1965 II:57: Since the parties of the deed did not have the intention to transfer the property but only to give the immovable object as security, the conveyance which was concluded according to the rules on transfer of ownership was declared void.

the present Real Estate Code, 'black price' expressed an amount which was not part of the written deed. In legal practice and also in literature, it was considered valid under certain conditions. The rule was, however, that the seller could not exact payment if it was based on an oral agreement. On the other hand, if such an amount was paid, it could not be claimed back on the basis that it was not legally valid. Thus, a written agreement about the price which is not part of the contract of conveyance may be valid *inter partes*, but it has no effect on the transfer of the ownership of the property.[57]

III. Terms and Clauses of Conveyance

A. *Clauses on Cancellation and Suspension*

329. A clause may be included in the deed of sale to the effect that the sale may be cancelled under certain conditions (condition subsequent).[58] Other terms may have the effect that the validity of the contract is dependent on a future event (suspensive condition). Both categories of terms are legally enforceable if written in the deed. In the event of a subsequent condition, the conveyance is normally valid but may be revoked at a later stage. In the case of a suspensive condition, the conveyance does not become valid before the occurrence of the specified event. If this event does not occur, the deed has no relevance, and the seller maintains his title. Registration of title is possible when the suspensive condition has been fulfilled.

330. The law provides for certain cases of cancellation of a contract, which are mainly related to fault or delay of the parties. In addition to these situations, the parties may agree upon other grounds of cancellation (REC Chapter 2, section 2). However, some categories of terms are invalid (see paragraph 334).

331. A suspensive clause may allow the seller to retain the title to the real estate until the price has been paid or another condition fulfilled (reservation clause). Another case of suspensive term is a clause that the buyer does not acquire the title before the death of the seller; these types of clauses may be used in a deed between parents and children. Suspension creates an interim regime in the title. The property right is described as being divided into the actual, ongoing right of the seller and the eventual, expected right of the buyer. The eventual right restricts the competence of the seller in the sense that he may not enter further legal acts which might affect the future rights of the buyer (mortgage, compulsory auction, etc.). One aspect may cause conflicts, namely the right to possession; does it belong to the actual or the eventual owner? If the suspensive clause is aimed only at protecting the seller's right to the purchase price, it is not obvious that the seller would have an interest in retaining possession of the property. The contract should, therefore, provide clarity over the party's intention regarding possession, not only the title.

57. See the Supreme Court cases KKO 1959 I:1 and KKO 1972 II:25.
58. In the previous stage of law, conditions subsequent were not permitted (*non-scriptum*).

332. A subsequent clause may be used, for instance, when a building lot has been sold with the expectation that it will obtain a building right at a later stage. If in fact the application of the buyer for a building license is refused by the authority, this offers a ground for claiming cancellation. But not all unexpected events afford this opportunity because certain risks lie with the buyer after the conveyance of the title. This is the case when new land-use restrictions are enacted by public law; for instance, a plan being ratified which limits the building rights. Also, other unforeseen restrictions, originating from conservation measures, may not be covered by contractual terms if issued after the sale. In addition to this, the buyer has the duty to explore the legal and real conditions of the object sold and take into account that a plan may be under preparation. A similar situation occurs when the municipality decides to exercise a right of pre-emption. A contractual retention clause would not be enforceable because the decision of the municipality to use its right has an immediate effect on the buyer's status; he loses his right to dispose of the property to the municipality which replaces the buyer in his position in relation to the seller (including all clauses of the sale document). As described below (see paragraph 493), the interference of the municipality may have some consequences for the fulfilment of contractual terms, e.g., concerning fixtures or the seller's right to use the property. However, a sale contract cannot limit a right of pre-emption as regulated by law. Even if some clauses of the sale would be 'personally' bound to the buyer and his performance, this is no reason to deny the right of pre-emption.

333. A clause, whether subsequent or suspensive, is not binding unless it has been incorporated into the deed of sale. Oral clauses are not binding. In order not to unnecessarily jeopardize the legal stability of property rights, a time limit for invoking clauses is set by law. A clause is supposed to remain enforceably valid for no longer than five years from the conclusion of the sale. If no validity period for the clause has been stipulated in the deed of sale, the clause is valid for five years. An action for the return of the real estate to the seller must at the latest be brought three months from the end of the validity of the clause. The act of return may be contractual or judicial. Since contractual cancellation of a sale means transfer of ownership, an agreement on the cancellation of a sale of real estate or the return of the real estate to the seller shall be concluded in accordance with the regular provisions concerning the form of sale.

B. *Void Clauses*[59]

334. The Real Estate Code provides for rules on inappropriate clauses in a sale contract. In principle, terms which may affect land-management or exchange of real estate in a negative way are void. For both parties, some clauses are invalid per se (*non-scriptum*, REC, Chapter 2, section 11).[60] Unless otherwise provided, the following clauses are not binding in a sale of real estate:

59. See Zitting-Rautiala, 282–299, Jokela, Kartio & Ojanen, 67–77.
60. For previous ruling, see Decree 1864 on inappropriate conditions in sale of real estate. According to this statute, a clause which left open the purchase price for further discretion of the seller was void.

335. (1) A clause under which the seller or a third party has the right to redeem the real estate at will or under which the seller or a third party has the right of first refusal before the real estate is conveyed to a new titleholder (clause of redemption).

- This provision must be studied in the context of terms on dissolution of the sale; they are, as described above, in principle permitted and binding. A non-binding term on redemption covers situations where the seller would have a rather open and indefinite right to dissolve the sale. Acceptable subsequent conditions are limited to five years, and the dissolution requires specific reasons. Thus, a term such as 'the buyer is entitled whenever he wants to redeem the property' is clearly in contradiction of the clause of redemption.

336. The reason for the ruling is to protect the buyer against non-predictable events which in turn might restrict his own right to dispose freely of the property (mortgage, lease, etc.). Also third parties (authorities, financial bodies, etc.) should be confident that registered real estate circumstances are stable and real. In practice 'sale and lease back' appeared before the entry into force of the Real Estate Code as a popular instrument for giving security to the seller. In this case the property is sold to a financial company which leases it back to the seller. The seller again may after fulfilling the debt 'redeem' the property. These terms are seen as not acceptable. The sale may also be void in the absence of an explicit term of redemption, when the intention of the parties according to the sale document is to give the property as 'interim' security only. Similar constructions may occur while concluding an additional 'pre-contract' which then, under non-pronounced terms, leads to redemption of ownership to the seller. The position of the legal practice therefore is that the needs of using property as security are satisfied in full by the mortgage legislation.

337. (2) A clause which restricts the right of the buyer to re-convey the real estate, to raise a lien over it, to agree on a lease on or other special right to it, or to otherwise dispose of it in a comparable manner.

- In this case, the term is aimed at limiting the buyer's sovereignty as owner of the property in favour of the seller or a third party. The reason, of course, is that after legal conveyance of ownership, there would be no reason to maintain any claims of the seller concerning the possession of the object. As mentioned before, the seller's interests (right to unpaid price or usufruct as part of the price) are accepted and legal. But in other cases, terms of sale may not lead to restrictions concerning the new owner's competences. Of course, other agreements establishing limited rights for the seller in addition to the sale are possible in a regular manner.

338. The prohibition in regard to a clause restricting the buyer's right to convey the property holds one exception. A clause to the effect that the buyer is not entitled, without the consent of the seller, to re-convey an undeveloped real estate or sell it below a set price, is binding. The objective is to prevent speculation in undeveloped land, especially in the case where a municipality or another public corporation has sold land with the intention that the buyer will develop it in accordance with the local building policy. However, such a clause is binding only if it is in writing and incorporated in the deed of sale. Also, the clause is valid for a maximum time of five years.

339. (3) A clause which limits the liability of the seller or a previous titleholder in cases of contesting of title.

- The legal provisions regarding the seller's liability for defects in the object or faults in the performance are binding, and terms limiting that liability are not binding on the buyer. A legal defect means that the buyer may later on lose the property to someone who proves to have a better right to the same than the seller (REC, Chapter 2, section 19). The buyer is entitled to claim for cancellation of the sale, return of the paid price, and eventually monetary compensation for losses based on fault. The rule regarding void terms applies also to predecessors of the seller. If the defect lies with a predecessor, the buyer who loses his title to the 'right' owner may also address his claims to that predecessor, instead of his contractual party, the seller (REC, Chapter 3, section 6).

340. On the other hand, a seller's liability may not be realized due to the buyer's action (see paragraph 383). If the buyer was aware or should have suspected defects in the object or did not appropriately investigate the conditions around the sale, his claim may not be successful. These rules are also taken into account in instances where a sale contract includes a void term regarding the seller's liability.

341. (4) A clause which restricts the personal freedom of the buyer or is otherwise improper or illegal.

- This is a general provision limiting the use of unacceptable terms. There is a close relationship to the rules in contract law which may imply that additional legal provisions in the REC would not be necessary. Terms which are not in accordance with good practice or principles of law are generally void, and a party cannot invoke such contractual terms.[61] The concept of being contrary to good practice is considered to have a broader range of application than simple illegality. A specified regulation in property law takes into account that family relations and other personal connections may require a more precise legal study of the circumstances where a deed has been concluded and of the need for protection for the party in the weaker position. The expression concerning personal freedom may be relevant if, for instance, a conveyance has been made on the condition of future marriage. Also, the sale contract could affect a party's right to choose the domicile. In addition, there are terms which might be averse to public law rules, for instance, a term under which the buyer undertakes to alter the property contrary to valid rules on site protection or on the use of resources.

61. Government Bill to the Real Estate Code (Hallituksen esitys Eduskunnalle maakaareksi ja eräiksi siihen liittyviksi laeiksi) 120/1994, 47.

342. This type of immoral or inappropriate, although perhaps formally still legal, clauses are, according to the doctrine, void only if a party invokes them. They are not taken into account ex officio because the grounds for consideration may be highly personal and even explicitly accepted as binding by both parties. If a case concerning legality of a clause is brought to court, the question about the implications for the contract arises: presently, the position seems to be that a demand of restitution could be successful if such a term is deemed to be unreasonable for the party under protection.[62]

343. Some terms are open to interpretation despite the rule that they are supposed to be void. Voidness is subject to decision of authorities even if ex officio. If, for instance, a suspensive clause would normally prevent registration until fulfilment of the condition agreed upon, the registering official may consider the clause to be void and enter the title of the buyer into the register without taking the suspension into account. In principle, all suspensive and subsequent conditions (for instance, a clause limiting the buyer's right to convey, point 2 above) may come under the light of void terms as soon as the buyer applies for registration. The recommendation, however, is that the official should hear the opinion of the parties before setting the term aside because the intention of the parties may not be obvious. If a dispute occurs, the issue may be brought before a court for decision.

C. Litigation of Unreasonable Terms

344. The REC regulates validity of contracts and terms but it does not provide for rules on litigation. Instead, the general rules of the Contract Act (Chapter 3) apply.[63] The Contracts Act opens the way for the adjustment of unreasonable clauses (section 36). According to this provision, a term may be adjusted or set aside if it is unfair or its application would lead to an unreasonable result. In determining what is unfair, the entire contents of a contract must be taken into account, as well as the mutual position of the parties, the prevailing circumstances at and after the conclusion of the contract. Further, other factors may be taken into consideration. If a term is such that it would be unreasonable to enforce the rest of the contract after the adjustment of the term, the rest of the contract may be adjusted or declared to be non-enforceable. Moreover, the price foreseen in a contract may be adjusted. As stated above, a 'black' or non-reported purchase price is not as such legally enforceable and hence not adjustable; however it does not bring about the voidness of the sale as an effect. Litigation concerning professional sale of consumption products is regulated specifically in the Consumer Protection Act (38/1978, Chapters 3 and 4).

345. In the case of void clauses, the theory has adopted the position that in court procedures, the authority may ex officio take into account the voidness of clauses and other stipulations, without assertion of the party, which otherwise would be

---

62. The other position would be that a claim for restitution would not be possible if the term is not just contrary to good practice or moral but also illegal.
63. REC, Ch. 2, s. 11 refers to s. 36 of the Contract Act.

required. The argument for this is that public interests, i.e., land-management, may need to be taken into account.

IV. Powers of Attorney

346. A power of attorney for a sale of real estate must be in writing (REC, Chapter 2, section 3). The seller must sign the power of attorney, which indicates the attorney and identifies the real estate to be sold.

A. *Sale in Name of Company to Be Established*

347. If a sale of real estate has been concluded in the name of a limited liability company to be established and the company has not become responsible for the sale within two years of its conclusion, or the establishment of the company has been discontinued before that time, the person concluding the sale in the name of the company shall be deemed the buyer (REC, Chapter 2, section 4). According to the Companies Act (734/1978, Chapter 2, section 14, paragraph 3), a deed may be entered in favour of a not yet registered company but the seller, knowing this, has the right to renounce the sale. In such case the seller will forfeit his right to renounce the sale if no action for the same has been brought within two years of the conclusion of the sale.[64]

V. The Notary Institution

A. *Organization*

348. The notary system lies under the supervision of the Ministry of Justice and, hence, is an activity within the public domain. Persons qualified to attest sale documents as notaries are appointed by Decree (Decree on Notaries 968/1996). Some civil servants are qualified on the basis of their profession, others based on an individual authorization or recognition. The first category is comprised of certain officials (e.g., in the registry, police, and land survey administration) and the second of individuals appointed by a court or the head of the administration in question. Furthermore, appointed persons must fulfil requirements concerning competence and tuition in legal matters. Persons acting as notaries are listed in a register kept by the Centre for Legal Registers, and the notaries are identified by given criteria. The register is open to the public in accordance with the Personal Data Act (47/1987).[65]

64. After the conclusion of a contract to establish a company, the registration must take place within six months (Ch. 2, s. 9 Companies Act). If this does not take place, the person who represented the planned company replaces the buyer in a sale of real estate.
65. In case of an attestation abroad, the Ministry for Foreign Affairs is entitled to enact regulations.

B. Attestation

349. The notary must, before entering the attestation, check the identity of the parties who have signed the deed and confirm that the legal formalities for a sale have been met. On request, the notary must verify that the information in the sale document regarding ownership, limited rights and easements is in accordance with the land property register and the real estate register. The notary must also, if the sale concerns only a parcel of a registered real estate, together with the parties and eventually using map material, identify the unit concerned. After the investigation, the notary attests the deed by his signature and registered identification. The attestation must also give information regarding the names of the parties as well as the place and date of attestation. Each copy of agreement must be attested individually.

C. Legal Effects of Attestation

350. An attestation of a sale has legal implications for third parties as well. For instance, it is a precondition for the use of the municipal right to pre-emption of the sold property. It also constitutes proof of ownership to be used for register and mortgage purposes as well as in land survey and planning procedures. For this reason the notary must, as soon as possible and in any event within seven days, inform the municipality and survey authorities[66] about the conveyance of ownership as regulated in detail in the Decree. The notary must also keep an archive and a public diary for the attestations. In his work, a notary takes liability as a civil servant for errors and faults.

VI. Pre-contract

351. The parties may conclude a contract of intention (pre-contract, preliminary agreement) on an intended sale of real estate (Chapter 2, section 7). In order to be binding on the parties and third parties the pre-contract must be concluded in accordance with the regular provisions on conveyance; in particular, the requirement of written form and attestation must be respected. If not, the contract only has effect as an obligation between the parties, not in rem. The pre-contract may be agreed to be binding on one of the parties only. This may occur in cases where one of the parties has a specific interest in the matter (e.g., the establishment of a building project).

352. The pre-contract usually has a limited duration. Accordingly, the pre-contract must indicate the deadline for the conclusion of the sale of real estate and the conditions whose fulfilment trigger the sale. However, the price and other considerations may be left to be later agreed on the basis referred to in the pre-contract. If the period of validity of the pre-contract has not been indicated, it shall be five years from the conclusion of the pre-contract.

66. This administration performs a further distribution of the information to other authorities. Ministries concerned organize together the dissemination of information.

353. In order to proceed to the final agreement, a party to the pre-contract has the right to bring an action within the time limit determined in the contract and demand that the other party shall conclude the sale as agreed in the pre-contract. Furthermore, a party shall have the right to due compensation for breach of pre-contract.

354. If the real estate has, during the validity of the pre-contract, been conveyed to a third party, this is held to be a breach of the pre-contract. Thus, the buyer referred to in the pre-contract is entitled to claim due compensation from the seller. In the event that the pre-contract has not been concluded as described previously (i.e., in the order provided for conveyance), the seller is liable if he withdraws from the sale but his liability covers monetary compensation only (REC Chapter 2, section 8). He must compensate the other party for the reasonable costs incurred by advertising, visiting the real estate, and other activities necessary for the conclusion of the sale. If a down payment has been made, the amount paid in excess of the costs referred to above shall be returned.

355. The principle of freedom of agreement governs the conclusion of contracts of sale. The seller and the buyer must fulfil their obligations as agreed (Chapter 2, section 9). There are, however, specific binding provisions in the Code, partly in order to protect the interests of the weaker party, partly for the maintenance of security in the registry system. Some of the legal provisions concerning the rights and obligations of the parties to the conveyance provided for in the Code may be explicitly excluded by agreement.

356. The law provides rules regarding clauses and terms which may be binding for an agreement. If the agreement contradicts these binding provisions, the law will eventually apply directly instead of the terms in the agreement. Since the buyer in cases of fault or defects in the object is the weaker party, his rights may be restricted by agreement in specific situations only. Thus clauses will not be enforceable if they limit the buyer's rights to react when faults or deficiencies later appear in the sold property or when third parties' rights would interfere in the sale. Generally, the seller cannot free himself from liabilities and obligations which might occur due to faults attributable to him. However, the buyer has a duty to obtain satisfactory information about the object – fault in doing this may prevent him from claiming compensation or any other sanctions from the seller, provided that the seller was not mala fide or did not conceal information.

VII. Specific Clauses Concerning Acquisition of Residential Real Estate from Merchants

A. *Legislation*

357. Professional sellers of residential land must respect specific conditions when selling real estate (REC, Chapter 2). This especially means that the seller may not rely on certain aspects of the agreement to the same extent as in normal cases of conveyance because he is supposed to have a professional knowledge of the contractual conditions. In addition, special rules apply to professional real estate agents. They may become liable for not having informed the buyer about all relevant features in the sale. The agent's liability does not limit the contractual obligations of the professional provider of land for the market.

B. Clauses for the Use of Services of Professional Merchant

358. If the buyer has acquired real estate to serve as a residence or leisure residence for himself or his family from a merchant who develops or sells real estate professionally, certain terms, if detrimental to the buyer, are not valid or binding. These terms are:

(1) a clause which derogates from the provisions concerning the buyer's right to withdraw from the sale or claim a reduction of price by reason of a defect in the real estate (Chapter 2, sections 17–34);
(2) a clause entitling the seller to invoke the time limit provided for a notice, in case of defect or fault (maximum of five years, Chapter 2, section 25, paragraph 2);
(3) a term that the buyer's liability for compensation may be adjusted, if late payment is a result of insolvency arising from illness, unemployment, or other special circumstance which is not primarily the fault of the buyer; and
(4) in order to limit the liability of the merchant, a clause according to which the seller is liable to compensate for repair costs, other necessary costs, and the costs of measures that have become unnecessary due to a breach of contract, if the matter concerns a hidden defect (Chapter 2, section 17, paragraph 1) or if the seller can prove that his conduct has been careful.

VIII. Effects of the Sale Contract

A. Seller's Obligation to Convey Real Property

359. The contract usually defines the date for conveyance. If the time of conveyance has not been set, the buyer has the right to gain possession of the real estate immediately after the conclusion of the sale. The real estate must be conveyed to the buyer on the condition that is to be deemed agreed upon (REC, Chapter 2, section 12). The seller must also hand over to the buyer title documents in his possession that are necessary for the registration of title since these documents are part of the object. The same applies to mortgage instruments, lease agreements, and other comparable documents that are necessary for the buyer as the titleholder of the real estate.

B. Right to Produce of the Object after the Sale

360. If the property remains in the seller's possession before the conveyance, the produce gained from real estate prior to the agreed time of conveyance belongs to the seller (Chapter 2, section 13). Use of natural resources is also permitted, but the seller may not take timber or excavate land resources in excess of the domestic use of the real estate sold, nor agree to attach special rights to the resources or the real estate. On the other hand, the buyer is not entitled to dispose of the real estate so that the use of the rights of the seller referred to would be precluded.

C. Conditioned Transfer of Title

361. In some cases a contract of sale does not have as effect the immediate transfer of ownership. There may be suspensive clauses in the contract itself, or other legal provisions may require a transitional period (right of redemption). The contract gives, however, the buyer some rights to dispose of the property until the final transfer takes place (Chapter 2, section 14). The buyer may after the conclusion of the sale use the real estate and dispose of it, as well as re-convey his right, even if the retention or transfer of title has in the deed of sale been made conditional. However, prior to the final transfer of title the buyer may not without the consent of the seller take timber or excavate land resources or other objects affixed to the real estate so that its value diminishes significantly. Furthermore, the buyer shall not raise liens over or attach special rights to the real estate without the consent of the seller.

D. Limited or Special Rights during the Conveyance of Title

362. In some cases third parties may have limited rights to the property under conveyance. If this right is a tenancy, the protection of the right is regulated by law. Here, the buyer must respect the existence of a tenancy, but he may under certain conditions give notice on the tenancy agreement (see Land Tenancy Act, section 12). In other situations of limited rights, the terms of conveyance should confirm the existence of such a right in order to maintain its validity against the acquirer. If the buyer is not supposed to know of the existence of a limited right or is not registered for a right of use, the right may not be enforced after the transfer of property. The rules, however, are not quite clear and vary depending on the category of usufruct.

363. The Supreme Court has in one case declared that even the awareness of the acquirer of the property right to a parcel that the seller had entered a contract to take gravel did not protect the contractual rightholder (KKO 1985 II:131), since there was not a clause in the deed of conveyance. The decision implies that all relevant terms should be indicated in the deed and that additional facts of reality should not be legally relevant. A similar situation was settled in Supreme Court judgment KKO 1992:57. Here the seller, A, had earlier entered an oral agreement with B allowing him to build a boathouse on the property. C who bought the property knew about this arrangement but did not approve it. B had to therefore demolish the construction.

IX. Liability for Public Debts and Risks

364. The seller is liable for debts and fees under public law and for other similar debts incurred prior to the conclusion of the sale (REC, Chapter 2, section 15). The buyer is liable for the stamp duty levied on the sale. If registered properly, these public fees are valid as statutory liens against later owners of the property (see paragraph 542).

365. There are specific rules concerning liability for risk of damage during the sale. Damage caused to real estate by fire, storm, criminal damage, or other reason not dependent on the seller after the conclusion of the sale shall be at the risk of the buyer, even if the seller retains possession of the real estate or the retention or transfer of title has in the deed of sale been made conditional (Chapter 2, section 16).

X. Liability for Faults and Defects and Lack of Information

366. A sale of property may consist of phases with varying obligations and rights. The entering into of a pre-contract and negotiations has been articulated above. The main topic is the validity of a sale and the parties' rights to invoke defects in the sale or its background information. Also, liability issues may occur after a valid sale. If, for instance, the object remains in possession of the seller, he may become liable for neglecting the management of the property.

A. Seller's Liability for Defects in a Sale

367. The law stipulates liability on the part of the seller for certain defects and deficiencies in the sold object. There are two main categories of defects, first, the substantial defect or the defect in quality and second, the legal defect or the defect in possession and title (Chapter 2, sections 17–19).

1. Liability for Defect

368. The criteria for a defect in quality are as follows:

(1) the characteristics of the real estate are not as agreed;
Supreme Court case KKO 1938 II:158: the claim for compensation was rejected due to lack of proof that the seller had assured the expected acreage of the building lot.

(2) prior to the conclusion of the sale, the seller provided the buyer with false or misleading information on the area of the real estate, the condition, or structure of the buildings, or other characteristic of the real estate pertinent to its quality, there being reason to believe that the information has had an effect on the sale;
(3) prior to the conclusion of the sale, the seller failed to provide the buyer with information on a characteristic referred to in subparagraph 2, which typically has an effect on the use or value of similar real estate and of which the seller knew or should have known, there being reason to believe that the failure had an effect on the sale;
(4) prior to the conclusion of the sale the seller noticed but failed to rectify the buyer's misconception of a characteristic having an effect on the intended use of the real estate; or
(5) due to a hidden defect, the real estate is of significantly lower quality than what can justifiably be expected in view of the price and the other circumstances.

2. Consequence of a Defect in Quality

369. In case of a defect in quality, the buyer has the right to a price reduction or, in a case of an essential or critical defect, to cancel the sale. Furthermore, in a case of a defect referred to in situations 1–4 above, the buyer has the right to due compensation.

3. Legal Defects

Legal defects are either defects in possession or defect in title.

370. The criteria for a *defect in possession* of a real estate are as follows:

(1) prior to the conclusion of the sale, the seller provided the buyer with false or misleading information on a current plan, building prohibition, conveyance restriction, or other official decision restricting the use or possession of the real estate, there being reason to believe that the information had an effect on the sale;
(2) prior to the conclusion of the sale, the seller provided false or misleading information on an official permit or decision relating to the use of adjoining real estate, there being reason to believe that the information has had an effect on the sale;
(3) prior to the conclusion of the sale, the seller failed to provide the buyer with information on a decision, or a permit, or decision in his knowledge, referred to in the law, respectively, which typically has an effect on the use or value of similar real estate, there being reason to believe that the failure has had an effect on the sale;

(4) prior to the conclusion of the sale, the seller noticed but failed to rectify the buyer's misconception of a decision referred to under point 3 above or a comparable circumstance, which prevents the buyer from using or possessing the real estate as intended;
(5) the necessary permit for a building on the real estate or for the activity carried out on the real estate has not been obtained; or
(6) a share or a parcel of the real estate cannot, due to the restrictions in the Real Estate Formation Act (1995/554, Chapter 4), be formed into new real estate or, when the share or parcel has been acquired for building purposes, into new real estate to be used as a building site.

371. As far as consequence of defect in possession concerns, the buyer has the right to a price reduction or, in case of an essential defect, to cancel the sale. As in the case of defect in quality, the buyer has also the right to due compensation.

372. The criteria for a *defect in title* to real estate are as follows:

(1) the buyer may lose title to the real estate in favour of the rightful titleholder, or the sale may be voided upon the request of a third party;
(2) prior to the conclusion of the sale, the seller provided the buyer with false or misleading information of the registered titleholder, a lien over, lease on, or other special right to the real estate in favour of a third party, or the ownership of a building, facility, or other object customarily affixed to the real estate, there being reason to believe that the information has had an effect on the sale;
(3) prior to the conclusion of the sale the seller failed to provide the buyer with certain information defined by law, there being reason to believe that the failure has had an effect on the sale; or
(4) the buyer cannot have his title registered if the title documents of the seller are defective or incomplete, or if there is another irregularity in the acquisition of the seller.

373. As a consequence of a defect in title, the buyer has the right to a price reduction or, in the case of an essential defect, to cancel the sale. Furthermore, the buyer has the right to due compensation. The buyer may also invoke a defect in title if a third party claims that he has a competing right to the property and there are likely grounds for the validity of his claim.

4. Defect in Providing Information

374. The seller has the liability for information concerning the object and the sale: in addition to his obligation to inform the buyer of all relevant facts concerning the object, he is liable for information provided by third parties. The seller is thus responsible for the information provided by a real estate agent or another representative acting on his behalf and also for the failure of such persons to provide information (REC, Chapter 2, section 20). Separate provisions are enacted on the liability of a real estate agent for compensation and on the information that a real estate agent or a merchant must provide when advertising real estate for sale.

5. Timing of Defects

375. Any defects in real estate will be determined on the basis of the condition of the real estate at the conclusion of the sale (REC Chapter 2, section 21). The seller is responsible for a defect existing at that time, even if the defect becomes apparent at a later date. The buyer cannot invoke a defect which the seller has rectified prior to the transfer of the possession of the real estate to the buyer.

6. Buyer's Knowledge of Defects (*mala fides*)

376. The buyer cannot invoke a defect of which he must have had knowledge at the conclusion of the sale (*mala fides*). The buyer is also, in cases of poor information, responsible for obtaining knowledge of relevant circumstances concerning the object and the sale in general (duty to investigate). If, for instance, the buyer has reason to assume that the property was used for an activity which may cause additional investments for his own activity (e.g., a need of reinstatement) he has the right to search for satisfactory information before entering the contract. Hence, the buyer cannot competently invoke a defect in quality which could have been noticed in an inspection of the real estate prior to the conclusion of the sale. However, the buyer is not expected to verify, without a special reason, the accuracy of the information on the real estate provided by the seller, nor extend the inspection to such circumstances where the inspection may require technical or other extreme measures (REC, Chapter 2, section 22).

B. Balancing

377. There are situations where both parties may have acted improperly and have breached their duties through negligence. In such a case, a court may balance the gravity of disregard or negligence of each party against the sincerity of expectations in order to find a reasonable result concerning the validity of the contract. As the buyer usually has a weaker position in terms of receiving knowledge of the object, he is protected even if he neglected his duty to explore the object, but it can be proved that the conduct of the seller had been in bad faith or gross negligence.

C. Seller's Liability after Validity of Sale

378. The seller may be liable after the sale, on the ground of fault, failure to perform, or delay (Chapter 2, sections 23–25). If he has, after the conclusion of the sale, neglected the appropriate maintenance of the real estate, wrongfully used it, or otherwise caused damage to it through negligence, the buyer has the right to a price reduction or, if the damage is essential, to cancel the sale (Chapter 2, section 23). Furthermore, the buyer is entitled to due compensation. The same applies if, after the conclusion of the sale, the seller wrongfully raised a lien over or attached a special right to the real estate. In order to enforce his right, the buyer must provide notice of the defect and of his claim based on it to the seller. This must be performed within a reasonable time after discovering the defect or from the time when he should have realized it. A notice is also required in cases where the buyer wishes to invoke a breach of contract on the ground of seller's fault.

1. Seller's Failure to Perform

379. If the seller does not fulfil a building obligation or other performance obligation connected to a sale of the real estate, the buyer is entitled to a price reduction or, if the failure is essential in view of the entire sale, to cancel the sale (REC, Chapter 2, section 24). Also, the buyer has the right to due compensation. What is stated above regarding the buyer's notice also applies here to the seller's failure to perform. If the buyer does not give notice of a defect in quality or a breach of contract or in failure of performance within five years from the transfer of the possession of the real estate, he will forfeit his right to do so. However, the seller will not be released from responsibility by virtue of lack of the buyer's notice if his own conduct has been in bad faith or grossly negligent.

2. Delay

380. If the seller does not transfer the possession of real estate at the time agreed, the buyer has the right to claim that the agreement be fulfilled (REC, Chapter 2, section 27). If the delay is essential and the buyer will not accept possession of the real estate, the sale may be professed as cancelled. The buyer also has the right to due compensation. The same rules apply if the seller fails to hand over the documents which are necessary for registration of the title or which concern mortgage, lease contracts, or other similar documents.

381. The buyer may, in addition, be guilty of delay. The buyer's main obligation is to pay the purchase price and to perform various other conditions. If he does not pay the price, a part thereof or other agreed consideration at the time agreed, the seller has the right to demand that the agreement be fulfilled and, in, addition, payment of compensation. If the delay is essential and the buyer does not pay the full price, the seller may cancel the sale and demand compensation, provided that it has been agreed in the deed of sale that the payment of the price is a condition of the retention or transfer of title to the real estate.

382. If the buyer's delay in payment is a result of a legal provision, an interruption in communications, or other similar force majeure, which the buyer cannot reasonably be expected to overcome, the seller does not have the right to compensation or to cancel the sale. The Interest Act (1982/633) applies to the right of the seller to interest for delay.

D. Buyer's Anticipatory Breach

383. In certain cases, it may become obvious before the sale has been completed that the buyer will not be able to fulfil his obligations. Therefore, even if the price or a part thereof has not yet become due and payable, the seller has under statutory conditions the right to cancel the sale, if it was agreed in the deed of sale that payment is a condition for the retention or transfer of title. Additional and optional conditions for this remedy are as follows:

(1) the buyer was declared bankrupt after the conclusion of the sale;
(2) the buyer was found to be without means in execution proceedings after the conclusion of the sale; or
(3) it is otherwise evident that the buyer will not fulfil his obligation to pay.

However, the seller does not have the right to cancel the sale unless the part of the price remaining unpaid is essential or if an acceptable security for its payment is given in a reasonable time after a demand for payment. Furthermore, if the sale is cancelled, the seller shall have the right to due compensation.

384. Concerning legal action in the case of breach, the REC provides for different modes of legal protection in cases of contractual misrepresentation by the parties (Chapter 2, sections 30–34). The ultimate remedy is cancellation of the sale.

E. Parties' Right to Withhold Performance

385. If the buyer has a claim based on the seller's breach of contract, the buyer may withhold payment of the price for the part corresponding to his claim (Chapter 2, section 30).

386. If the seller has a claim based on the buyer's breach of contract, the seller shall have the right to withhold possession of the real estate. If the seller has retained possession of the real estate, he may continue using the real estate as provided in section 13 of REC.

F. Price Reduction and Compensation

1. Price Reduction

387. A price reduction will be calculated by subtracting the value of the defective real estate at the conclusion of the sale from the agreed price. If the agreed price is not equal to the market value of the real estate in the agreed condition, the price reduction shall be calculated taking into account the ratio between the agreed price and the market price.

388. The seller is obliged to return the part of the price constituting the price reduction with interest in accordance with the Interest Act (section 3, paragraph 2); the said interest runs from the date when the seller received payment of the price.

2. Compensation

389. The legal requirement of due compensation for a breach of sale means full compensation for any damage resulting from a breach of contract. If the seller shows that a defect or a breach of contract referred to in section 24 of the REC (see paragraph 379 above) was not due to his negligence, the seller will not be held liable for compensation.

390. The compensation may be adjusted, if it is unreasonable having regard to the reason for the breach of contract, the opportunity of the party causing the damage to prevent it, the contribution of the other party, and the other circumstances.

G. Cancellation of Sale

1. General Rules

391. If the sale is cancelled, the parties return to the legal position as it was before the contract was entered into. The buyer must return the real estate to the seller, and the seller must return the price already paid to the buyer.

392. If the buyer has gained noteworthy profit or benefit from the real estate, he must compensate the seller for the same. The seller must pay a reasonable compensation to the buyer for the necessary expenses incurred for the maintenance of the real estate and for those practical investment costs that have added to the value of the real estate. The seller must return the price already paid with interest, as provided in section 3, paragraph 2 of the Interest Act; the said interest runs from the date when the seller received payment of the price.

393. The buyer has the right, within a reasonable time, to remove the buildings and facilities that he has built where these are not necessary for the regular use of the real estate and where their removal does not cause significant damage to the real estate.

394. A party may withhold his own return performance until the other party fulfils his obligations and pays the compensation and interest for which he is liable or gives acceptable security for their payment.

2. Restrictions to Right to Cancel

395. The right to cancel must be based on objectively acceptable facts, not for instance on a personal change of mind. Cancellation is thus a limited exception from the rule *pacta servanda sunt.* The buyer has the right to cancel the sale only if he can return the real estate to the seller.

396. A buyer who has attached a special right to the real estate, or whose activity or failure to act has decreased the value of the real estate, may cancel the sale only if he compensates the seller in an amount corresponding to the decrease in value. If the real estate is encumbered by a lien raised by the buyer, the buyer may cancel the sale only after paying the seller the amount recoverable on the basis of the lien.

397. The sale may not be cancelled unless pertinent action has been brought within ten years from the transfer of possession of the real estate. The provisions in this section are without prejudice to the right of the buyer to claim for his rights if his acquisition has been voided.

XI. Claim against Merchant and Developer

398. In certain cases, the buyer may address, instead of the seller, the professional merchant of the sale or a developer or producer of defective constructions or materials (REC, Chapter 2, section 26). These extensions of liability have their roots mainly in consumer liability. Thus, if the buyer has acquired real estate to serve as a residence or a leisure residence for himself or his family, he has the right, instead of claiming from the seller, to make a claim based on a defect in quality, against:

(1) a merchant who develops or sells real estate professionally and who has conveyed the real estate to the seller or a previous titleholder for the purpose referred to above; or
(2) a dealer of building elements, a developer, or other merchant who is responsible for defects to the seller or a previous titleholder by virtue of an agreement according to the Consumer Protection Act (Chapter 9).

399. A merchant is responsible as well, unless there is fault or negligence, for defects for which he would have been responsible to his counterpart, but only to the extent of his liability towards that counterpart. The merchant may be released from responsibility if the compensation for the defect has been paid to a previous titleholder of the real estate or if the titleholder has forfeited his right to invoke it by reason of failure to give notice of the defect. The buyer has to give notice of a defect that he has discovered and of his claim against the merchant.

399.1. The Act on Habitation Sales (843/1994) establishes liability of the professional seller especially in cases when the object is a building or habitation in the phase of planning or construction. The Act requires for instance that the documents concerning payments of the buyer as well as promises given by the provider are real and guaranteed. It also provides that the buyer must give his consent to changes in construction and financing arrangements affecting his rights and to pledge of shares in the habitation company. The buyer is entitled to claim damages for defects on different grounds, in some cases directly from the contractor.[67]

§2. REGISTRATION OF THE TITLE

I. Obligation to Register

400. The sale of immovable property is based on the general obligation to register a title (REC, Chapter 11). First, the law regulates the period for registration. This is of importance because the legal consequences of immovable property are connected to the registration. On the other hand, there are sanctions for neglected registration.

401. Second, as far as the sale is concerned, everyone must apply for the registration of title after having acquired real estate or a share or parcel thereof. Registration of title must be applied for within six months of the drawing up of the deed of conveyance or other document on which the acquisition is based, unless otherwise provided below. The same rules apply to donation and exchange of immovable property.

402. Inherited property, as well as property acquired in a matrimonial distribution, is subject to the obligation to register. In these cases, since there is no sale, the law has to set the time for registration. If title to real estate has been acquired by inheritance, the registration period begins when the estate distribution has become final. If no estate distribution is necessary for the acquisition of title, the registration period begins at the end of the period reserved for an estate inventory or, if a distribution of matrimonial assets is necessary for the separation of the real estate, when that distribution has become final. The registration period for an acquisition based on the distribution of matrimonial assets begins accordingly when the distribution has become final.

403. The registration period for an acquisition based on a will begins when the will becomes final or when the estate distribution or distribution of matrimonial assets becomes absolute, should one or the other be necessary for the separation of the bequeathed real estate.

404. If the acquisition is based on an official real estate formation measure, the registration period begins when the measure has been entered into the land register. If the real estate has not previously been entered into the land register, the registration period begins at the time of first entry. The registration period for an acquisition based on the decision of an authority not involved with the formation of real

67. The Supreme Court Decision KKO 2010:17/3.3.2010 gives an analysis of the criteria for the buyer's right to receive compensation.

estate begins when the decision becomes final. In the event that the real estate has been sold by enforced auction, the period for the registration of title begins when the deed of sale is handed over to the buyer.

A. *Exceptions from the Obligation to Register*

1. Cases

405. Title to State forests, expropriated units, lands separated for public use, accretions and relictions, common waters, and commons may not be registered. If such real estate or a share or parcel thereof is conveyed, the acquisition is subject to the obligation to register title.

406. If the titleholder of a real estate has not applied for the registration of his title within the period provided in the rules presented above, the registering authority may obligate him to do so within a set time limit under threat of a fine. If he fails to do so within the time limit, the registering authority may enforce the fine.

2. Registration pro forma

407. Registration pro forma is used for situations where the holder of the property is legally entitled to act as owner, but a registration would clarify his position. If, for instance, on the application of the owner of a real estate or a parcel of the unit has been formed in a survey procedure, his title to the new register unit needs to be registered because no acquisition took place. In order to update the information in the property register, he may apply for a clarifying or so-called pro forma registration (REC, Chapter 11, section 6, paragraph 2).[68] Moreover, if an owner which was a partnership company has been transformed into a corporation, there is no acquisition to register, but the new company may apply for registration.

408. In the event of a deceased person's undistributed estate, the heirs or holders of the shares are not yet owners of the immovable property in the estate. The registration is still in the name of the decedent. In order to clarify the situation, the heirs may together apply for the registration in the name of the estate. The final acquisition of the heirs will be registered after the distribution of the estate. Again, if real estate is jointly owned by several persons, one of them may transfer his share, but he cannot sell a part of the real estate before the unit has been distributed and partitioned. The reason for this is that before the distribution by contract or by partitioning, he would not have a determined area of the object in his possession. Until that, all parts of the real estate are jointly owned.

68. Sale of a parcel to someone else is under the obligation of the buyer to register even before the parcel has been separated to a unit. If, conversely, the owner of the original unit keeps the parcel and sells the basic real estate, he will automatically be registered as the owner of the parcel when the buyer applies for registration of his acquisition.

3. Registration of Title on Official Initiative

409. The exception to the rule that addressees of immovable property have to apply for registration is that the registration takes place ex officio in case of a sale of a parcel or a defined fraction (REC, Chapter 11, section 7). As said earlier, acquisition of parcels and fractions of real estate are under the obligation of registration although they are not yet separately formed as units in the land registry. These cases are systematically anticipated acquisitions of future registered units, but the reason for registration is clarity of the cadastre and the protection of the rights of the buyer. If the parcel or the fraction is later separated in a survey procedure, an updating of the registration unit is required. For this reason, the registering authority must, on its own initiative, amend the registration of title to a share or parcel of real estate to cover the real estate formed from it. This registration takes place after a newly formed real estate parcel has been entered into the land register. The person whose title to the share or parcel has last been registered is deemed to be the titleholder of the newly formed real estate.

410. The other situation referred to is parcelling or portioning of a real estate without selling parts or shares to others. Here the register authority may on its own initiative amend the registration of title to real estate to cover those new real estate parcels which have been formed. Appropriate objects for parcelling and partitioning on initiative of the owner are both real estate in general and also building lots in a city. A third situation is a change of the entitled owner by court decision, e.g., after a dispute. This amendment will also take place ex officio by the registering authority on the notification of the final judgment by the court.

B. Registration Procedure

1. Approval and Rejection

411. The administrative rules are enforced in the REC (Chapter 12). Some legal consequences of importance for the owners of real estate are connected to these procedural rules. It was already mentioned that neglect of a timeous application may lead to threat of fine. The handling of the application is formal in the sense that there is no discretion involved. The applicant for registration of title must present proof of the legality of his acquisition. The original document or a copy authenticated by a notary or a registering authority on which the acquisition is based must be attached to the application. An absence with severe consequences occurs where the title of the previous titleholder has not been registered. The later applicant must give this proof to support his own documentation. If the lack is not met, then registration cannot take place. He may succeed on a specific procedure which is based on public notice (see paragraph 414 below). There are also situations where the predecessor did not have to prove his title (e.g., public property). In this case the buyer has to give complementary proof. Proof is not required if the real estate under sale was obtained in a public auction or was formed in a survey procedure, including expropriation.

412. The application will be left undecided or suspended in certain cases. This indicates the formal role of the procedure (REC, Chapter 12, section 2). The reason for this in most cases is that the buyer or applicant has no full power to obtain the title. He may require the consent of a third party or of an authority, or there may be a term in the contract which is still open. Furthermore, a dispute in court may be pending, or the object was acquired by a company which was not yet registered as established. There are also some other cases. Usually there are time limits for keeping the issue pending. The decision on registration will follow depending on the development of the uncertain factors. If the proof with regard to the establishment of the company that was intended to get the title is not presented within two years of the conclusion of the contract of conveyance, the person concluding the contract in the name of the company will be registered as the titleholder.

413. The application will be rejected if it is not left in abeyance or if, after the specified time for pending has expired, the reasons for registration are not present (section 4). The reasons for rejections are that:

(1) no acquisition document or an authentic copy thereof has been presented;
(2) the acquisition document has not been drawn up as provided by law;
(3) no proof of the title of the conveyor or another previous titleholder of the real estate has been presented;
(4) the required consent or decision of a third party, competent body of a corporation, court, or other authority has not been obtained for the applicant's acquisition;
(5) the title to the real estate is returned to the conveyor because of a cancellation or suspension clause in the conveyance contract, and a judgment or agreement to this effect is presented;
(6) the real estate belongs to a bankruptcy estate, and this has been entered in the title and mortgage register prior to the acquisition; or
(7) the applicant's acquisition is otherwise not valid or will evidently not be permanent.

2. *Effects of Registration*

414. Registration of title by public notice is a remedy available to repair the lack of proof documents. The aim is to invite persons, by public notice, to present their eventually competing claims concerning the title in question. The remedy is available for certain deficiencies only and cannot be used for obtaining general confirmation of the title. The procedure is initiated by the registering authority if either:

(1) the applicant does not present an acquisition document or an authentic copy thereof, but he presents likely grounds for the legality of the acquisition; or
(2) the applicant shows that he or the previous titleholders have possessed the real estate as titleholders for the preceding ten years, and there is no reason to believe that another person has a better right to the real estate.

415. The registering authority issues a public notice and calls upon those persons who deem themselves to have a better right than the applicant to the real estate to make their claim before the register authority within six months of the publication of the public notice in the Official Gazette (*Virallinen lehti*). In addition, the public notice shall be notified to those known persons whose right may be affected by the registration of title.[69]

416. If no claim has been made or action brought within the set time limit, the application to obtain the registration of title may be granted. What is essential as far as repairing the lack of documentation is concerned, is the role of possession as a basis for getting the title: possession of ten years without contesting better rights entitles the authority to enter registration. In other cases, possession is no proof of title concerning immovable property. For land lease, the rule is that if the property has been leased to two persons, the first contract remains valid if the tenant has taken the property into possession.

C. Restriction of Owner's Powers

417. In civil law, restrictions to the transfer of property rights occur as exceptions from the freedom of contracts. Property may have been acquired under the condition that the owner abstains from certain contractual disposals, for instance, sale, establishment of limited rights, and more. The grounds for restrictions may be, for instance, in heritage or company law. In certain areas of land-use, the contractual terms may also limit the powers of the owner. This is the case, for instance, in planning law and conservation law.

418. To make these restrictions public, they will be entered in the register (REC, section 5). If a usufruct based on law or a will or a condition attached to the applicant's acquisition restricts the right of the applicant to convey the real estate, or to attach special rights to, or raise liens over it, the restriction of possession must be entered into the title and mortgage register at the same time as the decision in the registration matter is made or otherwise upon request.

§3. Contestation of Title of Ownership

I. The Problem

419. On the whole, the property register is a proof of title and objects of property rights. Under specific rules enacted by law, even those registered rights may be contested by third parties. The contestation implies that the petitioner, instead of the last buyer of the property, would be the entitled or 'right' owner of the title or the special right. The present legislation is based on the assumption that the person in whose name the title has been registered is the legal owner of the property. The contestation, therefore, has to bring evidence against this assumption. In some cases,

69. The procedure follows the court rules in Ch. 11, s. 10 of the Code of Judicial Procedure.

registration is decisive, but in others substantial reasons for contestation may be presented.

420. The protection of third parties' rights in the contractual sale of real estate requires special provisions in case the seller was not the legal owner, and the buyer might then lose the property to the legal holder of title (REC Chapter 3). The period of illegal or non-authorized possession of a property may also affect other rights which the buyer may have contractually or otherwise created during his ownership.

421. The principle is that illegal possession – meaning ownership which cannot be based on a legally valid chain of deeds – may not create a solid basis for the rights of third parties, whether this right is ownership or a special (limited) right. On the other hand, those right holders who may lose a right acquired in good faith may be indemnified by a reasonable compensation. Thus, a claim to keep the title of property may not be successful.

422. The 'rightful' holder of a title of a real estate is a concept that is used when a property has been illegally transferred to a buyer, which is, in theory, usually done in good faith. The criterion for defining who the legal titleholder might be is partly related to possession, partly to the registration of the previous owner's right.

II. Modes of Contestation

423. The rightful titleholder of a real estate may demand that the acquisition of the buyer be voided on the basis of a defect encumbering the acquisition of the seller and that the real estate be returned to the rightful titleholder (REC, Chapter 3, section 1). Conditions for a successful claim are enacted in Chapter 13 of the REC. The grounds for contestation are in line with the buyer's obligation to properly register his title to property (Chapter 13, sections 4, 5, 9, and 10). This obligation requires, *inter alia*, that the buyer provide sufficient proof of his predecessor's right to the title, and that the application for registration is presented in due time. Deficiency in this respect may open the way for a successful contestation by a person who gives proof of his better right.

424. First, there is the effect of a proper registration of the title. Since a deed of sale of immovable property requires certain formalities (REC, Chapter 2), a lack in this respect may lead to the invalidity of sale (see paragraph 400 for registration). However, a claim regarding a defect of form in the deed of acquisition will not succeed if the claim has been presented after registration of title based on it has been completed. Registration thus corrects a fault in form (Chapter 13, section 1).

425. Second, someone may contest the title on substantial grounds. In this respect, registration has no effect. Instead a dispute over the title to real estate or the validity of an acquisition can be raised in a court and, under specific conditions, in real estate formation procedure.[70] As described above, the applicant for registration may obtain protection if he can prove possession of over ten years without contestation.

426. If a dispute concerning title arises in an ongoing procedure, additional rules apply. Registration is not binding if competing claims concerning the title are raised in court or in a survey procedure. Courts and survey officials have the power to investigate the contents of a claim and decide the matter, at least as far as the case is concerned. A court decision may thereafter lead to amendment of the registration.

A. *Double Conveyance*

427. Special rules are provided for rare cases where the property has been sold twice. This occurs when the entitled owner (A) sells the property twice, each time to a different assignee (B and C). The objects may also be partly different, if for instance B buys the whole real estate and C a parcel of it. The rules on double conveyance apply to individual sales or transfers only and not to property units as heritage or immovable property of a company. Legally, both B and C may assume that A was the real owner but in fact he lost the competence to convey the object to C, to the extent that it was already transferred to B. Time priority is the main principle that applies for solution of the conflict between B and C (REC, Chapter 13, section 3). The first conveyance has priority because conveyances of immovable property are entered in the property register on the basis of the notifications by attesting notaries. This notification makes the acquisition public, and the second buyer C cannot therefore efficiently claim that he did not know about the right of B. In this respect, the validity of the registration of A has no relevance for the solution of the conflict between B and C.

428. But the subsequent conveyance of C takes precedence, if the registration of that title was first applied for by him, and he, at the time of acquisition, did not know nor should he have known of the previous, contested conveyance. The reason for this is that the second acquirer had no chance to know of the previous transfer if it has not been registered or notified by the notary. However, in the event that the first buyer had taken the object in his possession when the second buyer investigated the object, the latter buyer is then assumed to be *mala fide* and, therefore, cannot enforce his right by applying for registration. If registrations of title to several acquisitions are applied for on the same day by bona fide buyers, the earliest conveyance takes precedence. In the event that one application is rejected or a registered acquisition is invalidated or the conveyee otherwise loses his right based on the acquisition, the precedence lapses. The buyer who loses his right may sue A for breach of contract (legal defect, REC, Chapter 2, section 19, see paragraph 370 above).

70. According to the Real Estate Formation Act (s. 184), a dispute concerning property rights which occurs after opening the proceedings will be decided in the procedure by the officials. If the dispute was pending at the court, the survey procedure will be adjourned until the decision of the court is final.

429. The same rules apply analogically to donation, exchange, and other contractual transfer of real property. They also apply analogically to the relationship between property rights and limited rights and between limited rights. The time priority rule prevails. But if, in instances of registrable rights, the later entitlement had been registered first, it is protected. The situation is different in case of non-registrable rights. A conveyee of ownership, if bona fide, is not bound by a limited right established by a non-entitled previous owner.[71]

B. *Right Owner's Claim*

430. Occasionally real property is sold by someone (B) who was not the entitled owner. Specific rules regulate the conflict between the buyer (C) of such a property and the position of the original or right owner (A). The reason for this situation usually boils down to the lack of the registration of the title of B or some other circumstance (e.g., double sale at an earlier stage). The conflict between C and A who claims his right to be recognized, is based on certain rules (REC, Chapter 13, section 4). In principle, C can maintain his right if his title of the conveyor (B) was registered at the time of acquisition and the conveyee (C), at that time, did not know, nor should he have known that the conveyor was not the rightful titleholder. Thus, the registration of B, even based on false facts, corrects the defect in the title. A pending application on the basis of which a registration of title later takes place, has the same effect. This has immediate effect, also before the buyer has himself registered his title.

431. Accordingly, a special right to a lien over real estate is binding even if the person effecting it was not the rightful titleholder of the real estate, if his title was registered at the time of acquisition, and the person holding the lien or special right, at that time, did not know nor should he have known that he was not the rightful titleholder.

432. A person who has acquired real estate by inheritance, will, distribution of matrimonial assets, or means other than by conveyance does not enjoy the protection of good faith as described above (sections 3 and 4) against an earlier conveyee, holder of a special right, or the rightful titleholder.

433. There are, however, certain exceptions from the rule that registration of the buyer legitimates his title as conveyee when the seller was not the entitled owner.

---

71. A person in relation to whom an acquisition of real estate or a lien or special right remains valid (by virtue of REC Ch. 13, s. 4) has the right to due compensation from State funds. Also a conveyee or a person holding the lien or special right who loses his right to the real estate for the same reason has the right to due compensation from State funds. The right to compensation on a contractual basis of a person receiving compensation from the State will be transferred to the State from the amount of compensation paid. The Ministry of Justice grants and pays the compensation and represents the State in cases relating to compensation or recourse. The court shall on its own initiative notify the State when a case relating to title to real estate has become pending and may result in the State being held liable for compensation.

The reason for these exceptions is mainly equity or gross defect in the earlier chain of conveyances (REC, Chapter 13, section 5). The conveyee or person holding a title or special right does not receive the protection referred to before, if:

(1) the deed of title or other acquisition document of the rightful titleholder or the power of attorney or other competence document of his representative has been forged;
(2) the conveyance of the rightful titleholder is invalid because he had been coerced into it in a manner referred to in the Contracts Act (section 28); or
(3) the conveyor of the real estate or the establisher of a lien over or special right to it was registered as titleholder by mistake, or if the entry in the register was not based on a decision of the registering authority.

434. The buyer may also protect his title against the right owner on the basis of possession. In addition to the formal investigation of existing registrations of the title and their reciprocal priority, ongoing enjoyment of a property plays a certain role in decision-making (REC, Chapter 13, section 10). If there is a dispute regarding entitlement, and one person whose title to real estate was registered and who thereafter possessed the real estate for ten years – enjoyed as owner – that person remains the owner of the property. The requirement is good faith: it is assumed that at the time of acquisition he did not know, nor should he have known that the real estate had been taken from the rightful titleholder. As a result, and if no further action for a better right to the real estate is brought during this time, the rightful titleholder will forfeit his right to demand the return of the real estate.

435. An answerable subject in conflicts concerning conveyance is the person whose title has been registered. If he conveyed the real estate before the action became pending, the conveyee shall be summoned to answer in the trial. This rule applies also to claims for payment for real estate on the basis of a lien or directly by virtue of law.

C. Buyer's Protection against Enforcement

436. The owner of a real estate may not dispose of his title in cases where his legal capacity is limited. The reason for the lack of capacity may be execution against him personally, precautionary measure, provisional remedy, or bankruptcy. The conveyance initiated without capacity does not influence the right of the buyer to the property. Instead, the sale is valid unless the buyer knew or should have known that the seller was no longer competent to convey the real estate (REC Chapter 3, section 10).

1. Liability of Previous Titleholders

437. A buyer who has lost real estate through the contesting of title has the right to bring his claim pertaining to this against the previous titleholder in whose acquisition there has been a defect resulting in the voiding of the acquisition of the buyer, instead of against the seller (REC, Chapter 3, section 2). If the buyer has brought his claim against the seller, the seller has a corresponding right.

2. Buyer's Rights and Obligations

438. A buyer who has lost real estate through the contesting of title may retain the profit and benefits gained from the real estate if, at the conclusion of the sale, he did not know, nor should he have known that the seller was not the rightful titleholder (REC, Chapter 3, section 3). If the value of the real estate has decreased as a result of the buyer's activity or failure to act, he must compensate the rightful titleholder by an amount corresponding to the decrease in value, unless the payment of compensation is under the circumstances to be deemed unreasonable.

D. Liability of Rightful Titleholder for Compensation

439. The rightful titleholder has to compensate the buyer in a reasonable amount for the necessary expenses incurred for the maintenance of the real estate and, if the buyer at the conclusion of the sale did not know, nor should he have known, that the seller was not the rightful titleholder, also for those practical expenses that have added to the value of the real estate (REC, Chapter 3, section 4). The buyer has the right to remove, within a reasonable time, the buildings and facilities that he has erected where these are not necessary for the regular use of the real estate and where their removal does not cause significant damage to the real estate. The buyer may also retain possession of the real estate until the compensation has been paid, or acceptable security for payment has been given. An action based on sections 3 and 4 of REC must be brought within three years from the return of the real estate to the rightful titleholder through the contesting of title in court.

E. Restrictions on Acquisition

440. There are today very few restrictions on the acquisition of land, foreign citizens and companies included (Act on the Surveillance of Foreign Purchase of Land, 1613/1992).[72] In Finland, the purchase of real estate is, in practice, available to an alien, for example, foreign companies and people living abroad. In some regions, for instance, frontier zones, conveyance of real estate requires a permit granted by the environmental centre. A permit can only be granted under special conditions. A more general restriction applies to shores and other recreational areas: Here a foreign company or citizen requires a permit for acquisition of real property, if the property will be used for leisure or recreation. The purpose of this restriction has

72. See also Act on Surveillance of Foreign Purchase of Companies, 1612/1992. An alien owner must, as a rule, apply to the Ministry for Trade and Commerce for a confirmation of the purchase if the result would be a total of at least a third of the stock in the company.

been to keep nature areas free from constructions.[73] In reality, the pressure from abroad to purchase land for recreation has been rather unimportant. Nationally, a specific permit, in addition to the building license, may be required for building in shore areas beyond zoning areas.

§4. DONATION

I. Donation of Immovable Property

441. Donation of title to real estate or any parcel of land must follow the same rules as conveyance by sale. The rules on donation cover in principle the advancement of immovable heritage.

II. Donation of Movable Property

442. In principle, a fulfilled donation of movable property presupposes the transfer of possession. The act of donation consists of two elements, the promise and the transfer of possession. A promise must be in writing in order to have any legal relevance. A written promise to donate is not just a letter of intent. Rather, it is binding between the parties and the addressee may claim natural performance, i.e., transfer of possession. The promise has no effect against the creditors of the promisor or other holder of rights in his property.

443. The Donation (Movable) Act (625/1947) regulates promises and transfers of movable gifts. Essentially a donation is enforced in accordance with the tradition of possession to the receiver. However, a promise has certain legal consequences. An oral promise without transfer of possession has no effect unless it has been given in public with a clear intention to enforce the promise. The burden of proof of such special circumstances rests with the promisee. Again, if the promise is given in writing, either in a deed of donation or as a commitment in a letter of debt or sale, the promise is binding. This means that the promisee may claim delivery of the object in question. However, this right does not affect the creditors of the promisee as long as the donation has not been fulfilled.

444. The requirements for an act of fulfilment depend on the legal status of the object. Tangible objects must be transferred in order to fulfil the donation. The same applies to monetary promises. If a bearer's bond or a share document which is a proof of the right to the value invested has been donated, the promise is fulfilled by transfer of such a document. If the donation constitutes remission of a debt, the donation is not fulfilled unless the debtor receives the bond or document in question or it has been destroyed. For other financial documents, specific rules apply, for

73. According to the Government's Bill 120/1992, these restrictions are in conformity with the ruling of the European Communities on Member States' rights to restrict free movement of capital.

instance, registration of the donation or the remission of a debt in the official share register.

445. If, in other cases, the creditor has donated an obligation (claim) to a third person, the donation is fulfilled when the debtor has received notice of the act. The notice may also be given by the receiver of a donation as creditor if he is entitled to claim the fulfilment of the donation. If such a debt is remised, the donation is immediately valid. An act of donation may also constitute a deposition of money, shares, or other transferable financial documents. In these cases, the donation is valid if the deposition has been made or, if required, registered in the name of the promisee without the depositor's right to interfere in the use of the deposit.

446. Under certain circumstances, a donation may be withdrawn or reduced. This is the case when a binding promise has been made without transfer of the possession, and the donator's financial conditions worsen to the extent that expecting fulfilment of the donation would be obviously unreasonable. Also, when the beneficiary injures or violates the donator who made a binding donation, the donation may be cancelled as long as it has not been performed. If the donator becomes bankrupt, his creditors may claim withdrawal of the donation according to rules on recovery to the bankrupt's estate (Act on Recovery to Estate 758/1991) and the law on execution.

447. When dealing with donations to relatives, stricter rules apply in order to avoid simulated transactions. For immovable property, general provisions on conveyance, including the requirements of the deed being in writing and attestation apply. In cases of movable donation, however, donations must be registered at the magistrate (municipal administration) in order to provide protection for the beneficiary against the creditors of the donator. This is not required when the donations are reasonable in relation to the donator's economic situation.

§5. Other Contracts of Transfer *Inter Vivos*

448. Usually the object of sale is a registered unit, real estate. From the point of view of transfer, the same legal rules apply to all kinds of land and water areas, be it a unit or a parcel of real estate. The same is also true for objects under joint ownership. Other contracts implying a transfer of real property may be entered according to company law. Some cases of conveyance are not fully under the rules of the REC. The sale of share of a company which owns real property is not a sale governed by the REC. The same is also true for fusion and diffusion of companies. Moreover, transactions based on marriage and heritage law (distribution) are regulated separately. On the other hand, a capital contribution to a company, i.e., investing real property against shares, falls under the rules of the REC.

449. If real estate under joint possession is planned to be distributed among the owners, this may be achieved either by a survey procedure or a partitioning agreement. In the latter case a normal transfer agreement facilitates the procedure. In other cases, partitioning or distribution performed by officials in accordance with heritage and marriage law as well as law on surveying replaces the need of formally written agreements.

450. The provisions on the sale of real estate and the registration of the title apply, where appropriate, to exchange and gift of real property as well (REC, Chapter 4, sections 1–2). If the donee in case of donation breaches a condition relating to the use of the gift or another essential condition or prerequisite, the donor has the right to revoke the gift, unless the donee has conveyed the real estate to a third party. An action for the revocation of a gift must be brought within one year from the donor's gaining knowledge of the grounds for revocation.

451. In certain cases, conveyance of real estate may be part of a corporate settlement, for instance, an investment in kind in a company or as exchange for shares. In those cases, the provisions on conveyance of real property apply to a certain extent, where appropriate. This particularly means compliance with the formalities concerning conveyance by sale (REC, Chapter 4, section 4).

§6. Transfer of Limited Rights

452. Transfer of lease and usufruct is regulated under contract law. In addition, certain binding rules of the REC apply not only to conveyance of the title but also to the transfer of limited rights concerning land or water areas. This is the case if the area contains a building or a permanent facility or construction belonging to the usufructuary or if it is agreed that one may be built. Notably, these provisions concern the right to the profit of the land in question and the mutual obligations of the parties in case of negligence in filling the contractual or legal obligations, including compensation (REC Chapter 4, section 4). An agreement on the transfer of a registered usufruct and other limited rights must be in writing, and it must contain the necessary information for the identification of the contracting parties, the object, and other essential data. If the transfer is not to be registered and if either party demands it, the transfer must be made in writing even in other cases.

Chapter 2. Transfer of Property by Death

§1. Basic Rules

453. Death of a proprietor as a reason for transfer of a real estate is regulated by heritage law and, partly, by marriage law. According to heritage law, the estate is either subject to testamentary provisions or regular rules of estate distribution. If the deceased was married, marriage law affects the situation, depending on the contractual basis the spouses had agreed upon concerning their common property. The spouses may have property in common or may own property privately under a marriage settlement.

454. Under heritage law, the estate goes to the heirs according to the statutory order of succession, with the direct heirs being entitled to the legitim. Otherwise, the estate may be transferred by will without any legal restrictions. If the couple had no heirs, the estate goes, without testamentary provisions, to the survivor. The survivor also has, to the extent that he or she is not entitled to inherit, a right to dispose of the joint household of the couple during their lifetime. The direct heirs cannot claim partition of that part of the estate which comprises the common home of the deceased and the survivor.

455. The document of estate inventory[74] and the subsequent document on partition of the estate, both of which have to fulfil the formal requirements, replace, in the case of immovable property, the need for a formal deed of conveyance. After clearance of the obligations and securities burdening the heritage, the heirs and beneficiaries are entitled to claim division of the estate. At this point, the division may be agreed upon; otherwise the court may appoint an executor to perform the partition of the estate. If a property item awarded to one of the heirs is later on asserted and claimed by a third party, and the title is lost to him by court decision, the heir will receive compensation from the other shareholders of the estate.

§2. Heritage of a Farm

456. Specific rules apply when an inherited estate includes an agricultural farm. The purpose of the regulation is to keep a farm undivided where there are several inheritors, especially the direct heirs (Heritage Code, Chapter 25). The rules are not compulsory for the inheritors or the decedent, nor do they apply to areas where a zoning plan has been adopted. The ruling allows one heir or some of them to continue the farming activity and to satisfy the other inheritors with compensatory measures. The idea of farm heritage is the protection of the farm activity in the event of transfer to the next generation. The problem may arise that the farm unit would be split up between the heirs so that it no longer fulfils the criteria for public subsidies

74. This document is the basis for inheritance taxation.

or special treatment on taxation. Thus the distribution of the farm estate has a relationship to the rules concerning subsidies for agricultural farming, and the inheritor in question must fulfil the legal requirements for being acknowledged as a farmer in accordance with the national agricultural policy. This again is harmonized within the European Union (CAP).

457. The farm assigned to one part of the heirs does not constitute a separate property or capital; instead it will be distributed as part of the heir's share. If the value of the share is less than the value of the farm, the compensation to the other inheritors who lose their share in the farm and property under legacy may be financed by a loan mortgaging the farm. A farm may also be assigned to one of the heirs as an advance against his inheritance. Since in Finland farming is closely connected to financial aid and other financing instruments, the value of the farm may increase due to public support. If this is the case before the event of death of the intestate, the public support will be added to the share of the heir who received the farm as advancy. This regulation is partly a consequence of the reform of European CAP due to which subsidies are given to production units, not to the producers personally (the policy measures have been transposed into Finnish law through the Act 557/2005; the referred section 11 of this Act corresponds to the EC Regulation (EC) 1782/2003 Article 33).

Chapter 3. Possession

§1. *Usucapio*

458. *Usucapio* would mean enjoyment as a ground for obtaining the title. In real property law, the enjoyment is an element for solving a dispute on ownership. Possession alone is not sufficient for obtaining a title to immovable property. But enjoyment may be an additional factor for solving a dispute in favour of a non-entitled possessor of real property. According to general conflict rules, a requirement of proof for the registration of the acquired title is an unbroken chain of preceding titles (protection of acquisition). In cases of double conveyance, the priority of registration is primarily decisive (*prior tempore, potior iure*). In these contexts, possession has no legal function.

459. There is, however, a modifying rule on protection of enjoyment. According to this rule, a person whose title to real estate has been registered and who, thereafter, has possessed the real estate for ten years may keep the real estate, if he at the time of acquisition did not know, nor should have known, that the real estate had been taken from the rightful titleholder (REC Chapter 13, section 10). If no action for a better right to the real estate is brought during this time, the rightful titleholder will forfeit his right to demand the return of the real estate.

460. If the real estate has during the prescribed time been conveyed to another person, this person may also invoke the registration of the title and the possession of the conveyor and the good faith of himself or one of the previous titleholders at the time of acquisition.

§2. Acquisition *a non domino*

461. The lending of a tangible object is based on two main rules defining the holder's obligations (Commercial Code, Chapter 11). First, the person holding the object has to maintain the object so that it does not deteriorate. Second, the borrower may not use the object for any purposes of his own, such as pledge or other forms of security. The object must accordingly be returned in the same shape as it was received. The borrower may also not decide to transform the object into a pledge for a debt he has against the owner of the object; this would ultimately require the owner's consent.

462. If the holder has transferred the object contrary to the rules mentioned above to a person who is or is not aware of the legal status of the object, the owner is entitled to redeem it from the receiver. In cases where the receiver was acting in bad faith, the redemption goes without compensation.

Chapter 4. Accession

§1. Immovable Accession

463. Accession means connection of an object to another in a way that the attached object enters the existence and becomes part of the other object, both physically and legally. Rights to the receiving object also extend to cover the attached part. For this reason, it is not vital to look at the objects themselves but at the changes in legal rights the accession may cause. Often a contract is decisive for accession. A sale of real estate may or may not cover buildings or chattels. If, for instance, the owner of real estate sells the property to the tenant who has erected his own buildings (which are movable property and otherwise should be removed by the tenant), the sale rebuts so that the buildings become constituents of the real estate.

464. Accession concerning immovable property *de lege* is a rarity. Since immovable property covers all its constituents, one category of accession is the attachment of movable parts physically to a real estate. Someone, who is not the owner, may plant a tree on a real estate. The tree automatically becomes part of the immovable property. Constructions which have in a similar way been placed in the soil by someone else, for instance, illegally or a long time ago become constituents of the real estate and part of the ownership. A historical peculiarity is the rule concerning 'wandering islands' (Building Code 1734, Chapter 8, section 2 and Chapter 10, section 4). These were large turf rafts which broke away from land upstream and later on became stuck to land downstream. The accession rule brought that 'land' into the possession of the receiver without the possibility for the losing property to get it back. Also, when someone uses a field for cultivation without consent or agreement, the harvest can be deemed as property of the landowner.

465. In situations of usufruct and in contractual contexts, accession occurs at the end of the limited right. Within the contract, the holder of the limited right may have access to products which otherwise would be constituents of the real estate (vegetation, buildings, natural resources). The intention of a contract may be to give the holder of a usufruct or other right the power to use those products and to utilize them as the owner. Accession occurs when the owner of the property does not remove his property at the end of the term. In some cases, the landowner has the right or obligation to redeem property objects, especially buildings belonging to the tenant. The constituents created under usufruct and lease contract are then property belonging to the real estate under the accession rule. Similar rules and principles apply when the right of use is based on a license from an authority (private road easement, mining right, easements in general): after the end of the term, left-over constituents of the property legally accede to the real estate and become part thereof.

§2. Movable Accession

466. Accession of movable property occurs in two modes, combination and specification. Combination means that two objects are attached to each other, one of them being the essential part of the combined object. Parts added to a machine or equipment is a typical example. Usually the owner of the essential part will be the owner of the new object. But occasionally this is not so clear. One has to take into account the value of the attached part and the work invested in the combination. It is not impossible that a combined object has more than one owner; this might be the case, for instance, when a building is restored, and new embellishments, owned by someone else, have been added. Specification can be even more difficult to analyse. Usually it means that material has been transformed into an object, and there is a change in the ownership. Depending on the work invested and the difference in value between the material and the object, the owner of the result may be either the owner of the material or the creator of the object.

467. The conclusion requires an evaluation case-by-case. It is an accepted principle that a person who creates something new while using material belonging to someone else may become the owner of his work.[75] In the literature, it has been discussed what the role of bad faith on the side of the transformer might be. If he, for instance, has used material intentionally, knowing that he had no right to use it (it may have been stolen), then it might be unreasonable that the owner of the material suffers a loss. On the other hand, the value of the material might be insignificant in relation to the value of the produced object.

468. Furthermore, 'products' are also results of accession. Fruits of products may originate naturally or artificially. Human activities in order to improve or generate growth and fruits are comparable to specification. Nonetheless, the 'material' of transformation is difficult to locate in the product and, therefore, the fruits belong to the producer. Industrial products may have their origin in immaterial rights, but they are not 'material' in the sense referred to above (see paragraphs above 281–282). In practice, the most important regulatory issue concerns forest products. As constituent parts, forests and trees fall under the same regime as the real estate itself, as described above. Additional aspects arise in case of the growth of forests, which is the essential product. It is obvious that the natural growth is included in the concept of forests. The right to produce from forests may be transferred to others on different grounds. The separation or felling of trees leads to the question whether they belong to the property owner or the holder of a limited right. In the event of conveyance of ownership of the real estate, separated wood is the property of the seller.[76]

75. See, e.g., Heritage Code, Ch. 23, s. 11: An heir is entitled to get compensation from the other heirs for essential improvements in his share before the distribution.
76. In the judgment of the Supreme Court KKO 1953 II:19, the seller continued to manage the real estate after the sale contract was concluded. The court had to decide to whom the product of forests during this period belonged. The court stated that seller was entitled to a value corresponding to a reasonable calculated increase of product.

469. If a limited felling right has been established by contract, the ownership of the trees moves to the rightholder when the trees are separated. On the other hand, he also has the expectation to use forest products as soon as the contract is valid. The contract limits the power of the owner of the real property as soon as the right to the product – felled or not – has been transferred. The sale of felling rights may on the other hand decrease the value of the real estate. The general view is that the interim possessor would be entitled to limited use only, with domestic use being the benchmark. The parties to a sale may raise a dispute on the proper use of forest land and the effect of forestry on the value of the property. The burden of proof falls on the party who alleges negligence.

470. In heritage law, the situation concerning forestry is somewhat different. As long as an estate is not distributed, the surviving spouse has certain competences to use forest resources as well. A court decision stated that a widow was entitled to sell all the trees which could be felled according to an approved forest management plan.[77]

471. In addition to forest ownership, immovable property may also include other resources. In the Finnish system based on private ownership of waters, real estate may have water rights of economic value. The portion in rapids is a resource which can be sold or leased to a water energy company. Sufficient possession of water rights is required for the approval of a permit application.[78] The rapid rights acquired for a mill may be separated from the real estate they belong to and used as an economic resource. Private water rights are also required in other projects (bridges, waterways, harbours, etc.). These limited rights may be acquired by contract or on the entitlement of the water permit authority.[79]

472. As far as minerals are concerned, they are also constituents of real property. The owner is, due to the licensing system, not entitled to use the minerals or dispose of mining activities.[80] Some additional powers of the mining operator may also be established by contract (right to use roads, to fell trees, to excavate soil material, etc.). Otherwise, the decision of the mining authority, which in the end includes the formal mining rights, defines the relationship between the mining company and all the landowners concerned. The role of private land ownership is apparent from the fact that the operator has to pay an annual fee not only to the State but also to the landowners as a form of portion.

77. The Supreme Court's decision KKO 1937 II:352.
78. Water Act 587/2011, Ch. 8, s. 2.
79. Water Act, Ch. 2, s. 12.
80. Mining Act 621/2011.

Chapter 5. Occupancy and Dereliction

473. Occupancy means taking possession of an object without obvious ownership. The reasons for an object being without an owner are loss and dereliction. Only movable property can be lost and possessed by occupancy.

§1. Lost Property

474. The term 'finding' implies that an object has been lost unintentionally. Rejected goods are not 'lost' and cannot, therefore, be 'found' within the meaning of lost property legislation; those items fall under the rules of occupancy. Even if the original owner does not find the lost object, his loss of possession does not terminate his ownership. Therefore, lost property does not automatically become property of the finder. Finding or discovery is not a title per se. The public interest is to create a system where the finder has an interest to return unintentionally lost property, if possible, to its original owner. There is a need of incentive: primarily, the finder should return the object to a place where the owner may redeem it and eventually pay a reward. Only if the owner neglects this, the finder receives ownership by extinction of the original title.

475. The Lost Property Act (778/1988) applies to movable property but not to animals and objects under the obligation of registration (vehicle, aircraft). Certain items are regulated under specific legislation; thus movable objects are regulated by the Act on Protection of Antiquities (295/1963), objects found in shipwrecked vessels or in connection with rescue operations of ships (Maritime Act 674/1994), or objects under the legislation on rescue and return of spacecrafts (616/1970). The same applies to findings in connection with air accidents in accordance with the Aviation Act. According to these statutes, the finder is usually under an obligation to inform competent authorities about the finding without taking possession of it.

476. In cases under the Lost Property Act, the finder must, without unnecessary delay, notify the owner or deliver the object to the police. If possession of the object in question is forbidden or requires a permit from an authority, the object must immediately be delivered to the police. If the object is difficult to transport or transporting the goods may cause damage, the finder must inform the police without delivery. The police may authorize the finder to keep the object until further steps are taken. As long as the object is in the possession of the finder, he must take good care of it. However, if there is a risk of deterioration, the object may be sold if the police authority agrees to it.

477. If the object is found in a public area, for example, in a traffic area, station, office or hospital, the object must be given to the personnel of the institution (institutional finding). The same applies to authorized events that are organized outside for the public. The institution may keep the object for two weeks in order to allow reasonable time for the owner to retrieve it. After that, the object, unless it is insignificant, must be delivered to the police.

478. In situations where items of insignificant value are found outside institutions, the finder must inform the owner if he is known. If the owner is difficult to find, the finder may keep the object. The limit of value for such findings is presently EUR 20 unless the finder should understand that the object may have a specific value of use, sentiment or personal interest. In this case, regular behaviour is appropriate.

479. After a delay of three months from delivery to the police, the finder may take possession of the object if the owner has not claimed it. The finder is entitled to a reward which the owner has to pay before taking the object in his possession. The amount of the reward is defined by decree. Also, the costs for maintenance and transport must be paid to the finder and eventually to the office in question. In case of institutional findings, rewards are not foreseen. Ownership of objects passes to the State or the lost property office. Also, if the finder does not claim the objects found by him after a second delay of three months, ownership of the objects passes to those institutions as well. The finder cannot acquire ownership of bicycles and mopeds. If these are not redeemed by their owners, they will be sold at auction. The finder is, however, entitled to receive one-third of the selling price.

480. There are other objects as well to which the finder cannot obtain ownership. These are documents which can be annulled by their owners, products such as medicines, keys, credit cards, and other personal items, as well as objects for which a permit is required (e.g., weapons). If this property is not redeemed by the owner, it will be destroyed. The Act includes rules on the establishment and management of lost property offices; an administrative permit is required for these.

§2. Dereliction

481. Dereliction of an object gives the finder the right to take possession. The circumstances for deciding whether the object has been lost or abandoned may vary, but, in principle, the finder may take over ownership only if he is sure of the other person's intention to abandon the property. It is natural that only objects where possession proves ownership can be obtained in this way. Ownership of bonds and documents of value may not be transferable if the obligations are not bound to them.

482. From a public law perspective, there is a general prohibition against littering the environment. Waste law treats abandoned items as litter, and the person in question is liable for cleaning up the site.[81] On the other hand, the landowner may dispose of movable property left by others without regard to the value of the property for the owner; he may consider it as abandoned property and dispose of it.[82]

81. Waste Act 646/2011.
82. The case of the Supreme Court 1970 II:35: 'A metal company had sold real estate to the city. On the property, there was a heap of chrome residues. The municipality treated the material as waste and used it as landfill. The company claimed compensation for the loss of property values but the claim was dismissed.'

Chapter 6. Expropriation

§1. Legislation

483. According to the Constitution (2000, section 15) expropriation is defined as an administrative measure which, based on legislation, requires public need and, as a result, gives full compensation to the owner of real property. Here the 'legislation' means regular laws. If the taking would take place in a situation where there is no public need or where full compensation is not granted, there will be a need for constitutional legislation, i.e., an act which is adopted in the qualified legislative procedure of the Constitution itself. Those qualified acts are not part of the Constitution but involve additions to or exceptions from the Constitution as they may have a limited duration of validity. This constitutional order was more or less the same in the previous Constitution (1919). As a consequence, the Expropriation Act (603/1977) was enacted as a regular piece of law, based on the two basic limitations, namely public need and full compensation. For some specific situations of taking where these two criteria are not present, qualified legislation applies (e.g., Act on Expropriation for Electric Plants 168/1928: this act also applies where there is private need only – but still a 'rather' common interest).

484. The Expropriation Act applies in principle to all situations where there is public need for a taking. Nonetheless, there are still some exceptions in specific sectoral legislation. The exceptions may be either substantial (related to a category of projects, e.g., public roads) or formal (diversified procedure, e.g., in water law). The distinction between so-called statutory easements and expropriation titles is not always clear because the Expropriation Act applies not only to the taking of property rights but also of limited rights and to the setting of limited restrictions of use. In fact, the full name of the Act aims at 'expropriation of immovable property and limited (special) rights'. The difference between easements under the Real Estate Formation Act or the Private Roads Act, on the one hand, and the Expropriation Act, on the other, lies essentially in the fact that in the former case of easement, the right is established to serve existing property units. In the latter case of expropriation there is not such a need and the action may be initiated by applicants without any property rights in the area.

485. The Expropriation Act comprises a system of double decision-making. First, there is the need of a title to expropriate which is evaluated in an administrative expropriation permit procedure. Second, there is a survey procedure to enforce the expropriation, a procedure very similar to that under the Real Estate Formation Act. In this procedure, the object will be defined, the affected rights settled or annulled and the compensations prescribed on the basis of the value of the full property. The expropriation permit procedure vests in the State Government, with some exceptions. The survey procedure is conducted by a survey engineer, assisted by two laymen or trustees (expropriation commission). In most cases, a permit is required before the survey procedure may start, but there are some exceptions.

486. Expropriation has three functions:

(1) to acquire immovable property (ownership) or to obtain a permanent or temporary limited right therein;
(2) to restrict permanently or temporarily the right to use or to dispose of immovable property or a limited rights therein; and
(3) to annul a limited right (e.g., a lease or an easement).

The rule is that when ownership of real estate is expropriated, all other burdening limited rights will be annulled, since the holder of the title of expropriation is assumed to obtain full and unlimited competence over the property. Mortgaging interests will also be settled in the procedure.

487. The concept of immovable property comprises ownership or comparable unlimited possession of real estate or any part of land or water areas including buildings and constructions thereof. A limited or special right is a right to use or extract or an easement burdening immovable property, including buildings and constructions. If the land and the building thereafter have separate owners, the building is not part of the immovable property, but it is still in this context classified as immovable property. In such a situation, the compensation will be estimated separately for the owner of the land and the owner of the building.

§2. Expropriation Permit

488. As stated before, expropriation requires proof of a public need. This rule is complemented by an interest balancing rule according to which expropriation may not be carried out if there is an alternative to satisfy the need for compulsory measures, or if the negative effects of private interests exceed the profit of the public need. An alternative would, for instance, be the municipal right to re-emption or the conclusion of a land-management contract. What is important to notice is that private law corporations may also act on behalf of a public need, particularly so in the energy and traffic as well as the sanitation sectors. A private applicant also has to give reliable evidence that the project will be realized. This general ruling of public need (general title) is not used very often because the most common grounds of expropriation are stipulated in other laws (specified titles), especially the acts on land-use planning and construction of public roads as well as of other public traffic areas.

489. Expropriation for the establishment of nature preserves is also regulated separately in the Nature Conservation Act. Special laws do not, in these cases, provide for rules on expropriation other than the provision concerning the title. For this reason, the Expropriation Act applies to the permit and survey procedures as well as to the determination of compensation. In some limited cases, the competence to run the permit procedure is transferred from the Government to a ministry, usually the Ministry of the Environment. If there is an approved plan based on an administrative procedure, such a plan may supersede the need for a permit for expropriation and serve directly as a deed for expropriation. The same is true when a public road plan has been approved by the Road Administration. In some minor measures of taking, a separate permit is not required; instead the expropriation office (land survey administration) decides on the fulfilment of the requirements (public need, etc.) as well.

490. If the project for which expropriation is applied for would imply considerable impacts on the environment, an environmental impact assessment may be also required before approving the application. In these situations, the Environmental Impact Assessment Act (468/1994), which has been enacted in conformity with the EC legislation, applies. The Nature Conservation Act (1096/1996) may also impose mandatory restrictions or require additional approvals for the project, which the expropriation permit authority must take into account.

491. In addition, there are a number of laws within the character of expropriation. The Public Roads Act (503/2005) grants the National State Administration the power to acquire ownership of land for road purposes on the basis of an approved road plan. Similar powers apply for railways in accordance with the Railways Act (110/2007) and under the Aviation Act (1242/2005). Other legislation dealing with management of land and water areas may provide for a right to obtain an easement or a title of use if a project permitted by an authority would require that. Thus, the water permit authority may grant a permanent right to use land or water areas (Water Act 587/2011). A similar title of possession may be obtained for a mining company in accordance with the Mining Act (621/2011). In these cases, the position of the Constitution is that these titles do not fall into the regime of the constitutional protection of property since the property title is not endangered. If a water project is motivated by a public need, expropriation of ownership is feasible in the water permit procedure.

492. The enforcement of the expropriation and the determination of the object are tasks for the land survey administration. The expropriation committee is composed of three members, and the procedure is similar to other land survey procedures. The committee decides upon the object, and if limited rights are expropriated or restrictions set through expropriation, the committee will determine the content of the measures for registration in the land register. The register provides for information about different stages in the expropriation procedure. The expropriated property may normally be taken in possession after the legal force of the survey procedure and payment of the prescribed compensation. Under specific conditions, the right to advance possession may be granted. The committee also decides the seizure and compensations. Appeals are brought to the land court (division of the district court).

Chapter 7. Acquisition *ministerio legis*

§1. Redemption and Pre-emption

I. Public Law Provisions

493. Conveyance of land property may fall under the provisions of municipal right of pre-emption. Under specific conditions, a commune may intervene in a sale and claim to obtain the owner's right which the buyer would otherwise have achieved. The system prevents the purchaser from becoming owner, but the seller basically succeeds in his intent to the sell the property. According to the Pre-emption Act (608/1977), a municipality has a right of pre-emption in case of a sale of real estate within the municipality in question. The right exists if the municipality can prove that it intends to use the property for housing, recreation or conservation. This condition does not apply within the metropolitan area of Helsinki: here the city does not have to declare its intention concerning land-use.

494. The sale must be completed between the parties before the municipality can interfere. The parties may, before the sale is finalized, receive a binding answer from the municipality concerning the future use of the right of re-emption. If the answer was negative, this position is binding for two years and affords the buyer the right to become the owner. There are restrictions concerning the use of the right of re-emption. Some restrictions refer to the property itself, some to the individual parties, some to the selling price or the terms of sale.

II. The Object

495. A requirement on the first point is that the land area must have a minimum size over 5,000 m^2 (outside the metropolitan area, the limit is 3,000 m^2). If a sale between the same parties consists of several real estate parcels, the total amount of the objects will determine the size to apply. In order to prevent circumvention of the law, sales between the same parties during a period of two years in the same municipality will be considered in the calculation of the total area. If a sale covers real estate within different municipalities, the object will not be split up between the municipalities concerned. Instead, the municipality where the largest area of land is situated is entitled to pre-emption. This is due to the fact that only one municipality can enter the position of the buyer.

496. Since the right of pre-emption covers the sale as a whole and the municipality enters the buyer's position, the property may, in addition to real property, include movable property, such as machineries, stocks, and more. The situation depends on the contents of the deed.

III. The Parties

497. The second point refers to the parties. According to Finnish law, there is the freedom of conveyance. The parties may therefore be either physical or juristic persons, as well as private associations or public law authorities. A close relationship between the parties may prevent the municipality from using the right of pre-emption. This is the case when the parties are marriage partners or mutual statutory heirs. Also when the State or a State institution is the purchaser of immovable property, the municipality may not interfere. The same is true for property sold at a compulsory action.

IV. Price and Terms of Sale

498. When the municipality exercises the right of pre-emption, it must fulfil all terms agreed upon. In some cases, these terms may be too personal or specific for a third party to fulfil. If, for instance, the price essentially consists of items other than monetary units, the deed is an exchange rather than one suitable for pre-emption. If a term relates to the person of the buyer, the municipality may have to compensate the non-fulfilment of such a term with money, instead of fulfilling the term.

499. If a term or measure has been agreed upon between the parties, the purpose being to prevent the municipality from exercising its right to pre-emption, the court may, at the municipality's request, declare that such a term or measure is not binding for the pre-emptor. The request must be presented within three months after the confirmation of the deed.

V. Procedure of Pre-emption

500. After the confirmation of a deed of real estate conveyance by the attesting notary, the notary informs the municipality about the transfer. The municipality then, assuming that it fulfils the legal requirements for exercising its right to pre-emption, has three months to decide whether it will exercise that right or not. The decision must be made within three months after the confirmation of the deed. The parties, as well as the court of location, must be notified in order to make the decision valid. The parties to the sale may appeal against the decision of the municipality. A further transfer of the property or of a part of it during the pre-emption procedure does not prevent the municipality from exercising its right. Thus, for instance, the property which was originally sold to a person who was not a relative to the seller may, after receiving notice of the exercise of the right of pre-emption, be sold to the seller's spouse. Such a deed – as a regret – is irrelevant for the municipality's right.

501. The decision not to exercise the right of pre-emption is not subject to appeal. If the municipality does not follow the rules for exercising the right of pre-emption, the right will expire.

502. Since pre-emption does not legally alter the sale as a legal act, the municipality becomes party to that sale without any further deeds. When the decision concerning pre-emption is legal and valid, the obligations of the municipality are the same as in the deed. Should the original buyer have fulfilled some of those obligations, they are credited to the municipality, which again has to give compensation to the buyer. There are provisions regarding the mutual duties between the buyer and the municipality which apply in case the buyer either has invested in the property during the pre-emption procedure, or has used it in a way which caused damage or loss of value. The buyer essentially is obliged to take appropriate care of the property even if he will be replaced as owner by the municipality.

VI. Registration Issues

503. The real estate register provides information about the state of conveyance in the event of pre-emption. In cases where the municipality is entitled to pre-emption, the sale cannot be registered. After the passage of three months, the registration can take place unless the municipality has decided to exercise its right. Registration is possible at an earlier time if there is a decision not to exercise the right or the seller has received an advance statement that the right will not be exercised. If decisions concerning the right are open or appeals against them are pending, a registration of the original conveyance cannot take place either.

504. The decision to use the right of pre-emption will be noted in the register and removed when the procedure is over. When the municipality has fulfilled the obligations as the buyer, the municipality has the duty to apply for registration of conveyance according to general rules. The original deed which the municipality is entitled to receive from the original buyer serves as the necessary document for acquisition.

Part IV. Trust and Fiduciary Mechanisms

§1. Introduction

505. Entailed estate (fiduciary heritage) was a category of testamentary provisions with the aim to will the order of succession with binding force on the first and following heirs. Originally, the intention was to guarantee that valuable estates would remain in the family. This system limited the freedom of the heirs to dispose of this part of estate. In practice, this interim possession of heirs was not clear in the sense that full ownership as a rule would imply freedom of will. Entailed estate was therefore abolished in 1931.

506. In heritage law, direct heirs (children and their descendants as well as adopted children) are entitled to a lawful portion, in practice a half, of the estate. This right can only be set aside in very rare cases and not by testamentary provisions (Heritage Code, Chapter 7). If the deceased had no children, the estate goes to the surviving spouse. This right can be set aside by a will. In accordance with the Marriage Act, the surviving spouse may also have a marital right to the property of the deceased. This right may be excluded by an agreement between the spouses before or during the marriage (Marriage Act section 41). If there is no marital right, the surviving spouse keeps his or her share of the property according to the rules of possession in the Marriage Act, and the estate will be distributed between the holders of a lawful portion and other heirs in accordance with the Heritage Code (Chapter 23). Before the distribution, there will be an official registration of the property in the estate. This document serves as a basis for both taxation of the heirs and the individual portions assigned to the heirs. If the estate includes real property, the distribution document serves as a title deed for the property registration.

507. If the deceased had no heirs entitled to a lawful portion, then regardless of whether there was a marital right between the spouses or not, the surviving spouse has a specific right of possession of the estate.

Chapter 1. Administration of Property

§1. Introduction

508. There is no category of trust in the sense that someone's property would be under permanent restrictions, giving the decisive management power to a trustee. Property may, however, come under interim administration by a trustee under specific conditions. As a rule, these cases imply that the real holder of title has, for some reason, a limited power to use his competence, or that the person in question does not exist. In economic law, examples of these situations are found in bankruptcy law and in the law on execution. In civil law, the most common situations are guardianship of minors and absent people. The property of minors is not the property of the trustees but remains in the possession of those under guardianship. As far as minors are concerned, parents are, by law, frequently the guardians of their children. If a guardian has been appointed by a court to an adult, the court decides on the duration of the mandate.[83]

§2. *Fiducia cum amico* by Contract *inter vivos*

I. General Remarks

509. Property may be given as a deposit to others.[84] A pledge involves a deposition, but the main purpose is the use of an object as security. A deposit essentially means a deposition in order to allocate the property in a secure way without further intentions. This need occurs, for example, in connection with a removal. Between private persons, the contractual basis is rather free. A deposit is also a professional activity under the regime of the trade legislation. Here the contract is concluded in writing comprising the necessary terms on liability and maintenance.

II. Deposit

510. The deposit of movable property is generally regulated under the Commercial Code (Chapter 12), but in the event of a professional depositing, additional rules apply. In general, the following rules apply. A deposit agreement shall be entered into in writing or in the presence of a witness. Suitable items are variations of tangible objects from gold, silver and money to artistic objects and securities. The holder of the deposit is obliged to take care of it as if it were his own. In instances of negligence, the holder must compensate for the full value. If, however, the damage or loss is accidental, the holder is not liable.

83. Act on Guardianship 442/1999.
84. For deposit in connection to a service implying the right of the provider to retain an object, see para. 589.

511. The use or consumption of the deposit is not allowed without the consent of the depositor or the owner. If the object deteriorates, the damage must be compensated. If the object was illegally sold, pledged or lost, the owner may redeem the object from the receiver. If he is working under bad faith, the redemption goes without remuneration. If joint property has been deposited, one of the owners may not get it back without the consent or authority of all of the other owners. If this is not observed, the depositary is responsible for damage caused to the shareholders of the property. In turn, he may claim his debt from the owner who received the property without authority. The depositary may then, unless otherwise agreed, terminate the deposit and notify the depositor who is then responsible for the property. In the event of death of the depositary, the heirs are responsible for the deposit.

512. The depositor must pay necessary costs for management and rent before receiving the deposited property (retention right of the depositary).

III. Investment Funds and Pension Funds

513. Insurance companies, pension funds, and investment companies have, in accordance with specified rules, the possibility to invest their capital in bond securities and real capital. There are presently no general restrictions concerning the right to invest or the objects available for investments, but the activities of the companies are under public surveillance and State finance control.[85]

514. Insurance contracts are generally subject to the Act on Insurance Contracts (543/1994). Insurance operations and the supervision of insurance companies are regulated under the corresponding legislation on insurance companies (521/2008). These acts apply to the needs of indemnity insurance and personal insurance.[86] Nowadays, insurance may also have the function of investment. The Act on Pension Funds (1774/1995), created by employers, aims at guaranteeing the employees a pension and other benefits, without any profit to the fund. The investment strategy of the funds should lead to a sustainable growth of a secured capital.

515. The Act on Investment Funds (48/1999) applies to the operations of investment companies and deposit institutes. Fund investment is defined as activities based on the collection of investments from the public for purposes of bond security investments. The organization of the funds is composed of the general assembly of the holders of investment shares. The Act provides for rules concerning the principles of sustainable investments and the limitation of risks. The Act on Immovable Investments (1173/1997) applies to investments in companies with the objective of investing in real property. An immovable bond security entitles the holder to dispose of a defined part or share of real property. The establishment of a fund requires a capital stock and at least five members in the fund.

85. Act on State Finance Supervision 587/2003.
86. See also the Act on Insurance Associations 1230/1987, the Act on Employment Pension Funds 354/1997, and the Act on Foreign Insurance Companies 398/1995.

§3. *FIDUCIA CUM AMICO* IN THE FIELD OF SUCCESSORY LAW

I. Administration of Estates

516. Another situation is the administration of an estate if there is more than one heir. The Heritage Code provides rules for the interim management of the undistributed property (REC, Chapter 18). Principally, heirs, beneficiaries, and the surviving spouse are jointly entitled to manage the estate. The sale of a real property in the estate requires the consent of all parties. It is common, especially if there is a surviving spouse, that an estate remains undistributed for a long time; therefore the owners of the estate conclude joint transactions concerning the property. They may also jointly register their acquisition of title in the property register. The estate itself is not a juristic person and, therefore, cannot act as a party to contracts or in legal procedures.

517. The joint owners of an estate may apply in court for the appointment of an estate executor (Heritage Code, Chapter 19). A creditor may also apply for an order to ensure that the property is not dissolved by the shareholders before the official distribution. The appointed executor is entitled to represent the estate in all legal matters concerning the estate. However, if the executor intends to sell immovable property, the written and verified consent of the joint owners is required. A conveyance in conflict with this rule is void if a joint owner brings action within six months (Chapter 19, section 14). If the owners refuse to consent, the executor may ask the court to approve to the sale. The reasons for approval depend on the financial necessity of a sale to manage the estate.[87]

518. A surviving spouse has for social and ethical reasons a protected position in an undistributed estate. According to an amendment of the law in 1983, a surviving spouse may possess the estate undistributed (Heritage Code, Chapter 3, section 1a). This right is set aside if an heir with a lawful portion demands to receive his share, or if a will is contrary to the right of the surviving spouse. This situation concerns the estate as a whole. In addition, the surviving spouse has a better position concerning the possession of the common habitation of the couple. The surviving spouse is, against the rights and claims of other heirs, entitled to keep the common home under his or her possession. This is for practical and anticipatory reasons, such as if the surviving spouse has no other habitation available . If the estate includes several houses or apartments, one suitable habitation may be chosen. The right of the surviving spouse is legally a usufruct covering full possession and entitlement to return but not the right to sell the object (Heritage Code, Chapter 12). The usufruct limits the owner's right to use the object as security for the owner's debts. Debts of the deceased and of the estate may encroach on the rights of the heirs and hence also those of the surviving spouse. There are provisions concerning liability for poor management of property under hereditary usufruct. The same rules

87. See the Supreme Court Decision KKO 1984 II:223: the application was refused because the means could be found without selling real estate. The sale would also have been unreasonable.

apply to usufruct based on testamentary provisions. A will may, for instance, ensure the habitation of a person closely related to the deceased.

II. The Fiduciary Substitution

519. If an estate has several heirs, a surviving spouse and, eventually, other holders of rights to the estate, the heritage will be administered jointly, either by the inheritors themselves or an appointed administrator until the dissolution. During this period of time, certain measures may be taken individually by the surviving spouse or the inheritors, as far as they are required for the maintenance of the property or for the living in the joint estate. The intestate may also have given advancement or gift to some of the inheritors with the effect that it may lead to return if it exceeds the share of the person in question. At the dissolution of the estate, the changes and advancements will be taken into consideration for the final accounts.

520. If an estate includes a farm and one of the heirs is appointed to take over the activity, he may be obliged to give substitution to the other inheritors (see Paragraph 456). Also, if an heir assisted the testator in his living or professional conditions without a reasonable compensation, the person is entitled to a due compensation.

521. Successory reserves are addressed in certain cases. If the testator had young children, a certain amount may be taken from the estate for their education. The same applies to the parents of the testator if they are entitled to heritage.

III. Forbidden Testamentary Provisions

522. The criteria for acceptable testamentary provisions are basically formal or legal and not substantial. As a rule, all categories of private property are apt for testamentary disposal by a competent testator. Previously, during a categorization of patrimony and estate property, certain restrictions applied. In case of the involvement of marital rights of the spouse, some limits of disposal must be taken into account. A testamentary provision may be void if the testator lacked competence over the property in question, the formalities were not respected, or the testator was not capable of autonomous decision-making due to illness or if he was placed under pressure or other illegal conditions.[88] A testamentary provision is also invalid if it violates the right of an heir (his lawful portion). Most claims against assumingly illegal testamentary provisions are based on the circumstances where a will was signed.

88. Declared voidness of a will (Alzheimer): Supreme Court 2004:8/2.2.2004. The decision was reasoned on the basis of medical expert statements.

Chapter 2. Security *fiducia cum creditore*

§1. Fiduciary Juridical Rules

523. The Foundations Act (109/1930) applies to foundations or trusts as independent juridical entities. The establisher of a trust bequeaths a determined asset to be managed by a trust which, in order to have legal effect, must be registered in the foundation register within the National Board of Patents and Registration of Trademarks. After assigning the assets to the trust, the endower loses his competence to dispose of the capital invested in favour of the management board of the trust. The act of establishment of a trust may be a will or another explicit declaration. The Board approves the application to establish a trust before the registration. A trust only has economic purposes with a task of administering the capital and fulfilling the intentions of the trustor. Dissolution of a trust requires the approval of the Board as well.

§2. Sale with Clause of Selling Back

524. Under Finnish law, a clause of selling back is void, as far as immovable property is concerned. For 'sale and lease back' clauses, see paragraph 336 above. However, before the dissolution of such a contract, the regime may have caused legal consequences for third parties. For instance, the buyer may have concluded a lease contract or registered the property under mortgage. The validity of such agreements and transactions depend mostly on the good faith of the contracting party and the role of registration because certain limited rights are independent of the person of the owner.

525. The voidance of the sale between seller and buyer may also lead to claims for return of losses during the void possession. On the other hand, if both parties are *mala fide*, such claims may not be successful. If the property has been conveyed to a successor, general rules on protection of the 'right' owner's right apply. The bona fide successor may, under certain conditions, become the proper owner if his title has been registered properly (see paragraph 419).

Part V. Security

§1. Introduction

526. Security rights are largely used concerning financial security of both immovable property and retention interests in movable property. The establishment of security rights is related to the registration system of mortgages. In the case of movable property, possession may be a sufficient ground for security. However, many categories of movable property fall under the obligation of registration and, accordingly, the use of those items as security also requires registration. This is the situation, particularly in respect of vehicles, aircrafts, and vessels. In addition, certain collections of movable property – chattels or the inventory of a firm – may be registered and used as security. Some registered limited rights (usufruct) are also apt to be used as security for the purposes of the holder of the limited right. In order to achieve this goal, the contract of usufruct must fulfil some specifications (lease contract).

527. The mortgage of immovable property and land lease is regulated in the Real Estate Code (REC). The basic idea is that units and rights which have been registered as titles may also be used as security. The rule also works the other way around: immovable mortgages may only cover registered units and rights.

Chapter 1. Securities in Immovable Property

§1. PRIVILEGES, LIENS, CHARGES

I. Introduction

528. Security rights are classified as property securities and encumbered securities. In the first category, the creditor remains the owner of the security, and the seller retains the object as security for the unpaid purchase price (financial leasing). The second category, where the debtor is the owner of the object, is the most common, and it includes mortgage, pledge and retention rights. Promissory notes may be secured by a mortgage. Objects are as far as immovable property is concerned real estate, and certain limited rights, e.g., registered usufructs.

II. Immovable Privileges

529. Due to the uniform conceptualization of land property, all property rights of the same category are legally equal. In security law, privileges may occur in situations of competing titles of ownership. The law provides rules for solving conflicts in competence.

530. A privilege of another kind is the municipal right of redemption in the case of a sale of real estate. The use of this right may suspend the possibility for the buyer to use the property as security and also prevent the seller from taking measures, eventually foreseen in his favour in the contract (see paragraph 503). Rights based on expropriation are secured against interventions or claims originating from commitments of earlier owners of the property. There is no right of repurchase of expropriated land or property.

III. Securities in the Sale on Credit of Immovable Goods

531. The seller of immovable property may secure his right to the unpaid purchase price in two alternative ways, either by using a clause in the deed of conveyance or by applying for a mortgage over the property. Before the adoption of the Real Estate Code (1995), the seller was protected by a specific instrument of security, the so-called lien for reservation of the title, until the final payment of the purchase price. The effect of this was that the seller had priority over other creditors of the buyer from the date of conveyance.

IV. Real Burden in Joint Ownership of Blocks of Flats

532. A joint mortgage is a mortgage that is created over two or more parcels of real estate (REC, Chapter 16, section 2). This is possible on certain conditions, namely, when (1) the units belong to the same titleholder or the same titleholders in equal shares, (2) they are located in the jurisdiction of the same registering authority, and (3) they are not subject to mortgages, or they are subject only to mortgages for the same amount and seniority. These conditions imply that the real estate parcels must have the same legal status. A joint mortgage also has the effect that no further separate mortgages may be created over one or more of those parcels as long as they belong to the same titleholder.

533. A joint mortgage may be created over the entire real estate even if it is held in shares, because the object must be a legal unit, in this case real estate. But if in that situation, an agreement on joint possession has been registered and if a separate mortgage has already been created over a share of the real estate, the parcel may also be mortgaged. In principle, real estate is susceptible to mortgage. However, an urban building lot subject to a registered lease cannot be mortgaged by the owner. The reason for this is that the lease contract gives the leaseholder full competence to use the land and in practice excludes the owner of the land from the disposal of land-use. The owner's title is formal, rather than substantial.

§2. Mortgage of Immovable Property

I. Concept and General Features

534. A mortgage has a double function: first, to register limited rights over real estate and guarantee its validity against later successors or creditors of the landowner, and second, to create a lien for security over a property. The main requirements are that the mortgaged object is a registered unit in the property register and that the applicant has a reliable title to use the property as object for mortgage or lien (REC, Chapter 16). The regulation consists of rules concerning the establishment of a mortgage on immovable property (REC, Chapters 15 and 16) and those dealing with the establishment of a lien and the legal position of mortgage rights.

II. Subjects and Object

535. All immovable property units which are subject to the regulation of conveyance of real estate and other immovable property objects, for instance, a parcel not belonging to the titleholder of the real estate, are appropriate objects for mortgage and establishment of a lien (REC, Chapter 15). A mortgage may also be created over a share in jointly held real estate or parcel. A lien is the main category of mortgageable interest. A formal requirement for mortgage is that the title concerning real estate or parcel is registered in the property register.[89] In addition, statutory liens have by law a position within the mortgage register. Not only immovable property but also limited rights, registered with real estate, may be objects for mortgage

89. See the Supreme Court Decision Yearbook 1999:92: A and a Finnish bank agreed that an apartment in Spain owned by A would serve as security. When A later on sold the object he did not violate the right of the bank because the security was not registered according to Spanish law.

and lien. These rights are usually land lease and rights to utilize buildings. Formally, it is required that the lease or other right has been concluded for a limited period of time and that, according to the contract, the right may be transferred to a third party.

536. The titleholder of immovable property has the right to raise a mortgage over the real estate in question. The titleholder may also appoint an attorney to raise a lien. In the event of several successors, the titleholder who last applied for the registration of his title is entitled to apply for a mortgage over the real estate. If the title of the owner has not yet been registered, a mortgage cannot be established. However, if the application for registration of the title has been left in abeyance because of a contractual cancellation or suspension clause or because the real estate has been acquired in the name of a company to be established, the mortgage may be created on the condition that the conveyor of the real estate gives his consent to the mortgage.

537. The application for a mortgage must be in writing and signed by the applicant. The application must indicate the property to be mortgaged and the monetary amount of the mortgage. If the application aims at the creation of several mortgages over the same real estate, their order of seniority may be determined in the application. The titleholder of real estate may appoint an attorney to apply for a mortgage. The titleholder must sign the power of attorney, which also indicates the name of the attorney, the property to be mortgaged, and the amount of the mortgage.

538. A joint mortgage may cover two or more real estate parcels. The requirements are that the units have the same holders of titles, that they are registered in the same administrative region, and that the encumbrance of all mortgages over the real estate parcels is similar.

539. As far as validity of the mortgage is concerned, the legal effects of a mortgage begin on the day when the application has become pending. A mortgage remains valid until it is cancelled. A mortgage decision may be repealed or the mortgage annulled only if the acquisition of the applicant is not permanent; for instance, it may be valid for a limited period of time or otherwise conditional.

540. When the application for a lien has been approved and the mortgage registered, the applicant receives a mortgage instrument as a certificate of the mortgage.[90] There are, however, grounds for the application to be left in abeyance, e.g., in order to complete the necessary information; or for rejecting the application, mainly due to lack of authority to apply.

90. Upon notification, an entry must be made in the property (title and mortgage) register on the person holding the mortgage instrument. Where necessary, the register authority may require the holder to present the mortgage instrument (REC, Ch. 16, s. 9).

541. If real estate has been divided or altered in a land survey procedure, then, as a rule, the mortgage extends to cover all units formed from the unit under mortgage. However, if a lot was sold as a parcel before the establishment of a mortgage over the real estate, the mortgage does not cover the sold unit which was formed from that parcel. According to the rule on seniority or priority, a mortgage earlier applied for ranks prior to one applied for later. Mortgages applied for on the same day have equal seniority, unless otherwise declared by the parties on the basis of the application, when the mortgages are created.

III. Content of Immovable Lien

542. A real estate lien is raised by creating a mortgage over the real estate or other real property and handing the mortgage instrument over to the creditor as security for a debt. A mortgage instrument may be handed over as security of an eventual later debt. In this case, the lien will be raised when the debt becomes active. A real estate lien as security for the payment of a debt or fee under public law (statutory lien) is raised by entering it into the title and mortgage register.

543. The creditor has the right to enforce payment of the debt from the mortgaged real estate when the payment is due. The creditor also has the right to receive payment of a debt backed by a lien when the assets from the real estate are being distributed because of execution or redemption or otherwise by decision of authorities. The lien gives the debt precedence in accordance with the seniority of the mortgage, at most up to the amount indicated in the mortgage instrument.

544. The creditor has the right to enforce payment of the debt from the mortgaged real estate regardless of a transfer of title. The creditor may convey the mortgage instrument only if he at the same time transfers the debt which is backed by the lien. If the mortgage instrument has been handed over to a third party, the lien or second lien may be raised by the titleholder notifying the same to the third party, or by the lienholder presenting the titleholder's written certificate of the same to the third party. A mortgage instrument may not be taken in execution.

545. A debtor may commit himself to raise a lien. The commitment is legally binding and it entitles the creditor to demand that the titleholder hand over the mortgage instrument. In certain cases when the commitment cannot be realized the creditor may claim compensation. This is the case if the real estate no longer belongs to the person, who made the lien commitment, or if the mortgage instrument has been handed over to another creditor or if the person who made the commitment otherwise no longer has the power to decide over the lien.

546. In cases of sale of a parcel from real estate, the mortgage may change its limit. Thus, if real estate, subject to a joint mortgage, or a parcel of mortgaged real estate is conveyed to another person, the mortgage instrument based on the earlier mortgage may be handed over as security for a new debt. However, this is only the case if the mortgage has been lifted from the properties owned by persons other than the one raising the lien. However, the holder of the property title may hand over a mortgage instrument based on the mortgage of the entire real estate before the application is made for the registration of title on the acquisition of a parcel from that real estate. In such cases, the lien is supported only by the part owned by the titleholder.

547. Premature payment may be required under certain unexpected circumstances. If the security for the payment of a debt from mortgaged real estate is put in jeopardy because the value of the real estate decreases to an essential degree due to a fire, natural disaster, activity of the titleholder, or another comparable reason, the creditor may seek payment of the debt from the real estate even if the debt has not yet become due and payable. However, if the creditor does not bring an action for the payment of the debt within six months of gaining knowledge of those circumstances, he has no right to payment before the debt becomes due and payable.

548. The creditor has the right to receive payment from an insurance compensation before the debt has become due and payable. The holder of the title may, however, collect the insurance compensation if he has repaired the damage for which the compensation was paid or he has given security for the use of the insurance compensation for the restoration or repair of the damaged real estate. He may also collect the compensation if it is minor in proportion to the value of the real estate. If the debt supported by the lien is subject to a dispute or it is otherwise unclear as to whom the compensation should be paid, the insurer must withhold payment. Separate provisions apply on the right of a lienholder to compensation for redemption and compensation set in real estate formation procedures (e.g., expropriation procedure).

549. In cases of joint mortgage, a lien is backed in full by all real estate subject to a joint mortgage and all real estate formed from mortgaged real estate by parcelling, partitioning or surveying of an urban plot. If the mortgaged real estate belongs to different titleholders, the lien will be primarily supported by the real estate belonging to the debtor and thereafter by the other real estate, for the amount not recoverable from the primarily liable real estate. If several parcels of real estate belonging to different titleholders have been formed from one mortgaged real estate and the debt cannot be fully recovered from the real estate belonging to the debtor, or none of the titleholders is the debtor, the source real estate (the estate from which the parcels were separated) is primarily liable for the lien. There are more detailed rules about the order of liability of partitioned real estate and urban plots.

IV. Protection of a Lien in Cases of Conveyance and Execution

550. A lien over real estate remains valid even if the person raising the lien had conveyed the real estate before that time or if the creditor did not know, nor should he have known, of the conveyance. The creditor may not invoke his good faith if the information on the transfer of the title to the real estate was available in the property (title and mortgage) register for at least one month before the raising of the lien.

551. If the mortgage instrument has been handed over to the creditor as security for an eventual later debt, and the person handing it over had at that time the right to raise liens over the real estate, the lien remains valid, if the creditor did not know, nor should have known, of the transfer of title prior to the activation of the debt. The same provision applies if the creditor acted in good faith when receiving the mortgage instrument. In a case where the establisher of the mortgage loses his title due to a dispute on the right to the title, the mortgage he created during the period of possession remains valid against the new holder of title if the establisher had registered his title and the creditor acted in good faith regarding his right to dispose of the property. Depending on the situation, the State may be liable for damage caused to the new owner or to the holder of the mortgaged right because the registration of the title of the previous owner was false.

552. If, due to a clause in the deed of conveyance, the ownership of the buyer is revoked or otherwise annulled by reason of breach of contract or a court judgment, and the property is returned to the seller, a mortgaged lien raised by the buyer over the real estate remains valid.

553. A lien remains valid also if the holder of the title loses his right to the real estate through compulsory measures such as execution, precautionary measures or bankruptcy. This is not the case if the loss or limitation of the owner's competence was recorded in the title and mortgage register at the time of the raising of the lien, and the creditor otherwise did not know, nor should he have known, that the titleholder no longer had the right to raise a lien over the real estate.

554. If the mortgage instrument has been handed over to the creditor as security for an eventual debt, and the person handing it over had at that time the right to raise liens over the real estate, the lien remains in force unless the loss of that right was entered into the title and mortgage register prior to the activation of the debt, and the creditor did not know, nor should he have known, that the titleholder no longer had the right to raise a lien over the real estate.

V. Mortgage Alteration

555. Mortgaged rights may be altered in different ways (REC, Chapter 18). The seniority of mortgaged rights may be altered upon the application of the titleholder, if the lienholders and holders of special rights whose right decreases due to the alteration consent to the same. An alteration of seniority may also be effected upon the application of a lienholder, with the consent of the titleholder and the other holders or rights. The seniority of a joint mortgage may only be altered so that the alteration affects all the real estate equally. The seniority may not be altered so that a mortgage over only some of the real estate becomes more senior than the joint mortgage. A mortgage may also, upon the application of the titleholder and with the consent of the lienholder, be extended to cover other real estate belonging to the titleholder.

556. The merging and splitting of mortgages is also possible. Mortgages of equal seniority, or one mortgage following the other immediately in the order of seniority, as well as mortgages which follow each other but are separated only by the registration of a special right, may, upon the application of the titleholder and with the consent of the lienholder, be merged into one mortgage. The merged mortgage has the same seniority as the least senior of the original mortgages. In this case the amount of a merged mortgage may, upon the application of the titleholder and with the consent of the lienholder, be reduced so that it is less than the sum of the amounts of the original mortgages. Splitting of a mortgage is permitted on the application of the titleholder and with the consent of the lienholder into two or more mortgages, so that the sum of the amounts of the split mortgages is at most equal to the amount of the original mortgage. The split mortgages then have equal seniority, unless otherwise determined upon the request of the applicant.

557. A mortgage may, on the application of the titleholder and with the consent of the lienholder, be cancelled entirely or reduced to a given amount. The cancellation of a joint mortgage may be applied for by any of the titleholders of the real estate which are subject to the joint mortgage, even without the consent of the other titleholders.

558. If several parcels of real estate belonging to the same titleholder are subject to a joint mortgage, the mortgage may upon his application and with the consent of the lienholder be released in respect of a given real estate. The joint mortgage may not be dissolved, if the real estate remains subject to another joint mortgage. A joint mortgage over real estate belonging to different titleholders may, on the application of a titleholder and with the consent of the lienholder, be lifted from the real estate belonging to that titleholder. It is, with some exceptions, a prerequisite for such lifting that the titleholders of the remaining real estate and the holders of liens and special rights, of equal or less seniority over this real estate, consent to the same.

559. The mortgage instrument is void, and the lien lapses if the mortgage is cancelled or lifted. If the mortgage is altered as to its amount or the property which it secures, or otherwise, the lien will correspond to the altered mortgage.

§3. Mortgage and Lien on Limited Rights and Buildings

560. In order to protect right holders of usufruct against intervention by third parties, the right may be registered (REC Chapter 14). These registered rights may be used as objects for mortgaging and the establishment of a lien for a debt or credit (REC Chapter 19).

561. An appropriate object of mortgage is a lease and another fixed-term usufruct on the land of another person. It may be mortgaged if the right is transferable to a third party without reference to the titleholder. Another condition is that the areas contain a building or facility belonging to the usufructuary, or that it is agreed that one may be built (REC, Chapter 19, section 1). A mortgage may only be granted for a usufruct which is entered into the title and mortgage register. Also, a share of the usufruct may be mortgaged. One mortgage must be individually connected to one usufruct or one parcel of real estate. Two or more titles cannot be covered by one mortgage because usufructs and property rights may be conveyed separately.

562. The mortgage is created upon the application of the usufructuary whose right has last been registered (REC, Chapter 19, section 2). Registration implies that the applicant is legally entitled to the usufruct. Claims of priority will not be dealt with in the mortgage procedure. The provisions on mortgage of real property and establishment of real lien also apply, where appropriate, to mortgages over usufruct. If an agreement on the alteration of usufruct is concluded, the amendment is not binding on the lienholder before the registration of the alteration.

563. A lien over a usufruct lapses when the term fixed for the usufruct expires. However, the lien will remain valid if the usufruct is extended, or it is immediately given back to the same usufructuary, and an entry to this effect is made into the title and mortgage register during the term of the usufruct. If the usufruct expires prematurely because of termination, agreement, or another reason, the lien over the usufruct, as registered, remains valid until the mortgage has been cancelled. The same applies, if the holder of usufruct also becomes the titleholder of the real estate in question (merger). The lien remains valid if the creditor did not know, nor should he have known, of the lapsing of the usufruct at the time of the raising of the lien. In the case of a merger, the usufruct cannot serve as an object for mortgage.

564. If the titleholder has become usufructuary or the usufruct has otherwise lapsed, the mortgages over the usufruct may, upon the application of the titleholder and with the consent of the lienholder, be transferred to cover the entire real estate. In such a situation they have the same seniority as the registration of the usufruct and retain the same order of seniority as previously among themselves. It is a prerequisite for this that all mortgages over the usufruct are transferred at the same time. The lapsing of the usufruct does not affect the object of the mortgages over the real estate until the registration of the usufruct has been deleted. Thereafter, the mortgages over the real estate also cover the property previously subject to the usufruct.

§4. Statutory Lien

I. Legal Basis

565. A statutory lien means that a property is subject to liability for a debt directly by operation of public law, without the necessity of burdening the property with a mortgage (REC, Chapter 20). These situations occur mainly when the debt or a fee has its origin in public law. Public costs and payments arising from administrative measures on a property are often connected to the real estate and not to the owner who was actually the initiator or party to that measure. Those provisions can be found, for instance, in the legislation on land survey and forestry or land-use planning. In order to bind successors, the lien must be registered in the property (title and mortgage) register. The obligation itself is usually statutory. If the owner has been personally liable for the debt or fee in question, this personal liability does not pass to the new owner but is as a lien limited to the value of the property.

566. The subject of the obligation is not necessarily registered real estate. The same provisions on statutory lien apply also when the statutory lien covers an undivided share or parcel of real estate. Since special rights may also be registered to protect their continuity against third parties, these rights, namely a lease or another usufruct on the land of another person, are an appropriate object for a statutory lien. Thus, for instance, a lessee – more exactly his right of tenancy – may be liable for a statutory lien which has its origin in the tenancy. Otherwise, the real estate would have to bear the obligation. The same applies, for instance, to registered rights to use forest land or a gravel pit on a contractual basis.

567. A statutory lien gives protection to the public claim. If the debt or claim is not properly registered, it is still enforceable against the originator of the matter in question and his successors according to general rules on liability for obligations. Otherwise, a statutory lien must be notified for registration, i.e., to be entered into the title and mortgage register. If the notification has not been presented to the registering authority within one year from the activation of the debt, the lien will lapse (Chapter 20, section 2). The registration is not decisive for the validity of the debt. The registration does not prevent the parties to the obligation from challenging the validity of the obligation or the amount of the debt before the court.

568. A notification does not require that a debt be final. It may be made when the decision granting a loan or imposing an obligation to pay has been made, even if the decision is not yet final. A recurring payment from real estate, which is not based on a court judgment, may be notified for registration only if the payment of an instalment has been neglected.[91]

569. In case of statutory liens and the registration thereof, the provisions on real estate liens and mortgages apply, where appropriate (see paragraph 536 above). Some specific provisions will be presented here.

570. There are barriers to the registration of a statutory lien (Chapter 20, section 5). Thus, a statutory lien shall not be registered, if:

(1) the notification has not been made in the prescribed time;
(2) someone other than the debtor applied, before the notification, for the registration of his title on the basis of a conveyance, and he does not consent to the registration;

91. Detailed provisions on the notification and the minimum amount registrable as a statutory lien are issued by the Decree on the Title and Mortgage Register (960/1996, s. 21).

(3) an entry on execution or precautionary measures on the real estate or the bankruptcy of the titleholder has been made into the title and mortgage register prior to the notification; or
(4) the real estate is not liable in law for the debt, or the registration is otherwise not possible.

In cases of lack of information concerning the conditions of the debt, the notification for registration may be left in abeyance until the basis or the permanence of a statutory lien has been clarified.

II. Effects of the Registration of Statutory Lien

571. Registration has the effect that a statutory lien is valid from the date when the notification is properly made to the register authority (REC, Chapter 20, section 4). The registration has strong priority because, on the basis of a registered statutory lien, the creditor has the right to payment from the real estate before the payment of debts is backed by other mortgages. The same applies to interest, as registered, and other additional expense for a maximum of three years from the date of execution to the date when the interest is paid.

572. As far as the effect of conveyance and enforcement on statutory lien is concerned, there are limits to the binding force of a statutory lien on the holder of the title in cases of conveyance of the property (Chapter 20, section 3). There are two criteria: first, the statutory lien will not be binding on the conveyee if the lien was not entered in the title and mortgage registers before the conveyee applied for registration of his title of ownership (prior registration rule); and second, it is required that the conveyee did not know, nor should he have known, of the debt or the basis for it (bona fides). If he knew of the public commitment, e.g., having been informed by the seller, the lien is binding on him even if its registration was later than his registration of the title. The conveyor is also obliged to inform the conveyee of a debt payable from the real estate. If he fails do so and the statutory lien loses its validity towards the buyer, the creditor of the public debt has a right to due compensation from the conveyor.

573. Similar rules of prior registration are applicable in cases of execution, precautionary measures or bankruptcy. A statutory lien has no effect on creditors of the titleholder, unless it was entered into the title and mortgage register before the register authority was notified of the execution or other compulsory measures.

574. When the debt or claim in question has been settled, the registration terminates. The holder of the statutory lien must request that the registration of the statutory lien be removed when the debt has lapsed or when the lien is no longer valid. If the holder of the lien does not perform his duty, the registration may also be deleted upon the request of the titleholder, the actual owner of the real estate, or the tenant of a limited right to the property.

§5. Assignment of Mortgage Credit and Sale of Mortgaged Estate

I. Permanence of Registrable Limited Rights

575. If a limited right, for example, a mortgage, has been established prior to the conclusion of a sale and is registrable, the right remains binding on the buyer (REC, Chapter 3, section 7). As a rule, a registrable special right which has been attached to the real estate by the seller after the conclusion of the sale is not binding on the buyer. Certain conflict rules may, however, lead to the loss of the right.[92] Other limited rights are binding on the buyer of real estate only if he knew of the special right at the conclusion of the sale. If the holder of a special right loses the special right through a sale, he has a right to due compensation from the seller.

II. Position of Mortgaged Property

576. A mortgage does not restrict the transfer and the use of objects in a business activity in accordance with regular practices of exchange, renewal and development. Property which has been sold within this framework ceases to be part of the mortgage. If the merchant sells his trade or property, the business mortgage remains in force and has priority over a business mortgage of the conveyee of the property for six months after the date when the holder of mortgage was informed about the sale.

577. If a conveyed property includes business property in the mortgage, the acquirer may take responsibility for the mortgaged obligation on condition that all property under mortgage has been conveyed and that all holders of mortgage give their consent to the transfer of the mortgage. The buyer must apply for the transfer within three months after the sale. Similar rules apply in a situation where a European company[93] is merged with another company outside Finland, or the domicile of a company is transferred from Finland to another European State. In circumstances that involve the division of a company, the mortgage may be partitioned between the new corporate bodies with and in accordance with the consent of the holder of the mortgage.

92. REC, Ch. 13, s. 3, para. 3.
93. Council Regulation (EC) No. 2157/2001 of 8 Oct. 2001 on the Statute for a European company (SE), Art. 2, s. 1.

Chapter 2. Securities in Movable Property

§1. Privileges, Liens, Charges

I. Movable Privileges

578. Mortgages regarding trade property have been described above (see paragraph 304). A mortgage may also be used as security. In principle, this category of security may only apply to objects which are not applicable objects for other securities, for instance, immovable mortgage. One exception is a vehicle mortgage: the amount of a sale price which is not required for the vehicle mortgage may be used as security for the business mortgage. Also, if the business mortgage was registered before the owner of the business acquires ownership of the real estate of the location, the business mortgage remains in force. Otherwise, according to usual rules, the business property would become part of the real property and thus not constitute separate property. This has the effect that the holder of the business mortgage has priority against later mortgage creditors of the real property. However, this exceptional arrangement is only valid for six months after the business mortgage creditor has been given notice of the acquisition of real property. Objects under a business mortgage may not be given in possession of other creditors as a pledge, and such a pledge is not binding for the holder of the mortgage. The does not apply to bond securities and receivables.

579. The property under mortgage does not require identification because all movable property, both originally within the business and later on introduced, is subject to the mortgage. The object may, however, be limited to a specified part of the business property. The mortgage takes effect from the moment of registration of the secured promissory note. Priority commences when the application for registration is made to the authority.

580. In the event of the death of the merchant whose property is under mortgage, the burden passes to the property in his estate. If an insurance benefit covers mortgaged property, the benefit is the part of the mortgage as well.

581. In certain situations, the holder of a mortgage may claim payment before due date. These situations are related to negligence on the side of the debtor or risk of loss in fire or under similar circumstances. Such a claim must be presented within three months after the event in question.

II. Securities in the Sale on Credit of Movable Goods

582. In circumstances that involve instalment purchase, where the price is paid by instalments, the ownership of movable property remains with the seller until the price has been paid (Hire-Purchase Act 91/1966). Possession of the object is transferred to the buyer at the moment the contract begins. A contract which is aimed at conveying the title to the possessor is considered to be subject to the Act as well as in cases where the contract was for certain reason named as lease or usufruct. The sale contract must stipulate the amount of interest and other costs; otherwise these cannot be claimed. If the buyer neglects the payment of rates to a legally determined degree, the seller has the right to initiate a procedure in order to regain the possession of the object. In this procedure, a settlement of accounts is performed and the object taken back by the seller. For social reasons, the executor may postpone the procedure for a certain period of time.

§2. Pledge

I. Introduction

583. Movable security is based either on a pledge or registration of movable property. Retention is legally comparable to a pledge, but its purpose is different. All movable property is suitable for a pledge, but as far as registered property is concerned, additional measures are required in order to establish security.[94] A pledge is closely related to possession. A third party may, however, not always know what the legal basis for possession is. Therefore, rules are necessary to control so that the possession by the pledgee does not give the impression that he is the owner.

II. Pledge with Possessory Transfer

584. A pledge has two elements, the promise of a pledge and the transfer (*traditio*). The promise is binding without transfer of possession in the sense that the addressee of the promise may claim transfer of possession and, if this is not successful, compensation.[95] He has no right to take possession against the will of the promisor because the transfer of possession for a pledge is a contractual act. However, without possession, the pledgee has no protection of his right against creditors of the promisor. They may use the promised, but not transferred, pledge to satisfy their own demands. He also has no means to realize the pledge in the hands of the promisor or his creditors. Possession, therefore, in the case of pledge has a comparable position to that in sale. There are some differences due to the need to make a pledge perceptible to third parties. For instance, in the event of a sale of movable property, *constitutum possessorium* would be possible; the pledge remains in the possession of the promisor on the basis of lease or other contract, but for a pledge this is not satisfactory. For a pledge, the possession of the pledgee needs to be direct.[96] The pledgee may transfer the pledge as a (secondary) pledge of his own; in

94. A specific act applies to a pledge given as security for a third person's credit (Guarantee Act 361/1999).
95. If someone wants to pledge gold, silver and any movable property, he shall do it in the presence of two witnesses or obtain a certificate (Commercial Code, Ch. 10, s. 1).
96. See the Supreme Court decision Yearbook 1998:131: A and the company B had agreed that B would receive in pledge the fixtures located in the company C which A owned. Since the object was not transferred into the possession of the pledge, A did not violate the right of B when he sold the property of C to a third party.

this case the owner of the object must be notified. The pledgee is responsible for reasonable care of the object.

585. There are situations where the object may be in the possession of a third person – for which there may be several legal reasons. In order to create a pledge obligation, the pledgee receives indirect possession to the object by notifying the possessor in writing (possession based on notification, Commercial Code, Chapter 10, section 1). The possessor is in this case a third person.

586. The pledgee is entitled to realize the object under certain conditions. The most relevant requirement is that the debt is due and that the debtor has been notified in advance. If there is a risk that the pledge would lose its value as security, realization is already possible earlier.[97] In the event that the pledge consists of shares which give the right to possess an apartment which the debtor uses as his residence, a period of at least two months after the notification should be given for settling the debt. This provision is binding (Commercial Code, Chapter 10, section 2).

587. In case of a bond, possession of the document is not proof of the obligation. According to the Bonds Act (622/1947), a debenture is also enforceable without the bond. Instead, a bond is set under pledge by giving the debtor a pledge notice (section 31). The same applies to a pledge of share and similar value documents in cases where the obligation is not connected to the document itself.

588. For economic activities, a pledge which requires transfer of possession is not reliable because possession may indicate property or pledge, and eventually other limited rights. For this reason, needs of security to a larger scope are met with registration of the lien. This applies, for instance, to movable property in stores and means of transportation. It is, however, still acceptable to set a limited space under pledge.[98] Furthermore, reservation of the creditor's right in contract brings sold property under pledge until the debtor's obligation has been fulfilled.

§3. Retention Right, Compensation

I. Introduction

A. Retention Right

589. Movable objects may be retained as a security for a payment (Commercial Code, Chapter 12, section 12). Systematically retention is an exception from the

97. If the creditor as pledgee is a merchant, he has to inform the debtor about the realization of the pledge and the conditions on which the payment is recoverable from the pledge. This also applies to all securities concerning immovable and movable property. Other agreements are void.
98. In the Judgment of the Supreme Court Yearbook 1927 I 67, the pledge was considered to be fulfilled when the creditor received the key to a store, and the key was in his possession only.

prohibition to rely on self-help.[99] If an object has been produced or repaired according to an order of the client, the performer of the work is entitled to retain the object as security for the order until the debt has been paid. This right is effective only if the object is still in the possession of the creditor. Since retention is not comparable to a pledge, the retained object cannot be realized in the same way as a pledge. However, manufacturers are entitled to sell an object which has not been redeemed within six months.[100] In other cases, this right to realize the object does not exist. A creditor may retain any available movable property if the client owes payment for food or rent for habitation or vehicles.

590. There are some other retention rights to mention here. A landlord is entitled to retain movable property as a security for unpaid rent debts. This right applies to both the lease of land and to the rent of houses.[101] The retention may only cover debts and costs which are due to payment or will be due in six months. A depositary may retain deposited property for costs due to the management and care of the deposition.[102] A finder has the right to retain the finding as security for the finder's reward.[103]

591. Typically, the retention right concerns movable property. There is still one situation where immovable property may be retained as security. In this case, the buyer of real property has lost the title due to a claim of the 'right' owner. The owner has to compensate the buyer what he has invested in the property as improvements, assuming that he was not *mala fide* about the ownership. As security for these costs, the buyer may keep the object in his possession until the costs have been paid or a security deposited. In practice, possession means that the rightful owner cannot successfully evict the buyer who was not the entitled owner (REC Chapter 3, section 4).

B. Compensation

592. In cases of compensation or set-off of mutual obligations of two parties, the compensation may be settled against each other to the extent that the two parties have the same content. If, for instance, A owes EUR 1,000 to B and B owes EUR 500 to A, A may use EUR 500 as set-off and pay the remaining amount in money. Set-off is not a regular instrument for payments; instead, it is available in situations where one or both of the parties so require. Set-off gives the party with a greater interest the possibility to enforce his obligation by mutual compensation of the debts.

99. Zitting & Rautiala, 85 et seq.
100. Act on Manufacturer's Right to Sell a Retained Object 20 Jun. 1952.
101. Habitation Tenancy Act, s. 50, Land Lease Act, s. 20, Habitation Share Company Act, s. 15.
102. Commercial Code, Ch. 11, s. 3.
103. Lost Property Act, s. 3.

593. In Finland, there is no specific legislation on set-off, but it is practiced in case law. There are two categories of set-off, one voluntary and the other mandatory. Voluntary set-off is based on an agreement between the two parties; in case of mandatory set-off, the consent of the other party is not required. The latter is more common. In order to receive protection for the claim, it is useful to inform the party of the intention to set-off as soon as the conditions are fulfilled. Set-off is effective as soon as the party has been informed about the claim. The acknowledgement should preferably be in writing.[104]

594. All debts cannot be compensated, and set-off cannot be performed in all situations. In cases of mandatory set-off, there are three basic requirements. First, the claims have to be of the same legal character (e.g., monetary debts); second, the parties must mutually be equal parties of the debts or obligations; third, the debts have to be mature for collection and, hence, due for payment. Immature obligations may not be compensated, with the exception of bankruptcy. However, it is not required that the mutual obligations mature at the same time or that they are otherwise interrelated. The Bankruptcy Act (120/2004) gives a creditor the right, under certain conditions, to use his undue obligation for set-off (Chapter 6, section 1). This does not concern banks and other financial institutions where the debtor has account assets. Also, certain debts with a weak position in the bankruptcy proceedings (gift promise, debentures) do not fall under this ruling.

595. A debt which is statute barred can be used for set-off under specific conditions only. According to the Limitation Act (728/2003, section 15), obligations become statute barred within three years. A barred obligation may, however, be used for set-off in a case where the conditions existed when the acknowledgement to the debtor or the administrator of his property was made, or the debts originated from the same legal relationship (e.g., sale).

§4. Direct Claim

596. The concept of a direct claim would cover situations of recourse or recovery when a third person may interfere in the relationship of two persons. These situations occur, for instance, in relation to insurance agreements, lease and sublease, as well as security arrangements. A landlord may be entitled to a direct claim against sub-lessee or a victim against the insurance company of the policyholder. Since the right to bring a claim as a rule is given to the contracting party, situations of external claims are usually an exception and require specific rulings. To mention some of these situations: according to the Business Lease Act (482/1995, section 17), the subtenant is liable to the landlord for damage he caused, as if the sub-lessor had a lease contract with the landlord. According to the Consumer Act (38/1978, section 20), only the buyer and a member of his family may bring a claim against the provider of a product which caused damage or loss. According to the Insurance

104. In case a set-off claim involves a disputed debt, the existence of that debt shall be clarified in the same civil procedure: Supreme Court Yearbook 2007:25/15.3.2007.

Contract Act (543/1994, section 68), a victim of an incident may bring a claim against the insurance decision of the company.

597. Recent legislation on group claims opens the possibility for consumers to bring joint action against a liable seller or provider (Group Claim Act 444/2007). The legislation does not, in spite of certain political pressure, cover environmental liability which is regulated according to the principle of strict liability (Environmental Liability Act 737/1994). Strict liability is interpreted in the sense that it may open a possibility to make the operator of an installation liable, not only for operational activities, but also for damage caused by external repair and service providers, perhaps even by illegal actors in the territory of the operation.[105]

105. Supreme Court Yearbook 2011:62/31.8.2011.

Selected Bibliography and Legal Sources

Chapter 1. Literature

§1. General Works and Monographs

Aarnio, Aulis. *Perillisen oikeusasemasta* [*The Legal Status of the Heir*]. Porvoo 1967.

Aarnio, Aulis & Urpo Kangas. *Suomen jäämistöoikeus I-II* [*Finnish Law on Heritage I-II*]. Juva, 2000.

Haataja, Kyösti. *Maanjaot ja talojärjestelmä* [*Real Estate Formation and Register System*]. Helsinki, 1949.

Havansi, Erkki. *Kiinteistöpanttioikeus uuden maakaaren mukaan* [*Immovable Security According to the New Real Estate Code*]. Jyväskylä, 1992.

Hollo, Erkki J. *Erityinen kiinteistöoikeus* [*Law on Real Estates*]. 2nd edn. Helsinki, 1984.

Hollo, Erkki J. *Maankäyttö- ja vesioikeus* [*Land and Water Law*]. Helsinki, 2006.

Jokela, Marjut, Leena Kartio & Ilmari Ojanen. *Maakaari* [*Real Estate Code*]. 5th edn. Helsinki, 2010.

Kaisto, Janne & Tapani Lohi. *Johdatus varallisuusoikeuteen* [*Introduction to the Law of Property*]. Helsinki, 2008.

Kartio, Leena. *Esineoikeuden perusteet* [*Introduction to Property Law*]. Helsinki, 2001.

Ljungman, Seve. *Om skada och olägenhet från grannfastighet.* Uppsala, 1943.

Mattila, Heikki E.S. *Les successions agricoles et la structure de la société.* Helsinki, 1979.

Tepora, Jarno. *Johdatus esineoikeuteen* [*Introduction to Property Law*]. 2nd edn. Helsinki, 2006.

Tuomisto, Jarmo. *Omistuksenpidätys ja leasing* [*Retention of Ownership and Leasing*]. Vammala 1988.

Wirilander, Juhani. *Maanvuokraoikeus* [*Law on Land Tenancy*]. Jyväskylä, 1993.

Wirilander, Juhani. *Rasitteesta maankäyttömääräyksenä* [*Easement as Land Use Provision*]. Vammala, 1979.

Zitting, Simo & Martti Rautiala. *Esineoikeuden oppikirja* [*Textbook on Property Law*]. 5th edn. Vammala, 1982.

Zitting, Simo. *Omistajanvaihdoksesta silmällä pitäen erityisesti lainhuudatuksen vaikutuksia* [*Transfer of Ownership*]. Vammala, 1951.

§2. ARTICLES AND NOTES

Kartio, Leena. *Toisen maalla olevan rakennuksen pysyttämisoikeudesta ja lunastamisesta [Right to Retain Building on Someone Else's Land and Redemption]*. Turku: Yearbook Iurisprudentia Turkuensis, 1986.

Tepora, Jarno. *Reservation of Title as Security and in the Administration of Property*. Yearbook Scandinavian Studies in Law, 1985, 215–231.

Tepora, Jarno. 'Kiinteistöleasing – omistusoikeuspohjainen vakuusjärjestely' ['Immovable Leasing – Security Based on Ownership']. *Journal Defensor Legis* (1989): 354–380.

Zitting, Simo. 'Omistajan oikeuksista ja velvollisuuksista' ['Rights and Obligations of the Owner']. *Journal Lakimies* (1952): 387–401 and 1952, 501–531.

Chapter 2. Legal Sources

§1. LEGISLATION

Administration Act (Hallintolaki 434/2003).

Administrative Jurisdiction Act (Hallintolainkäyttölaki 586/1996).

Aircraft Mortgage Act (Laki kiinnityksestä ilma-aluksiin 211/1928).

Antiquities Protection Act (Muinaismuistolaki 295/1963).

Arbitration Act (Laki välimiesmenettelystä 967/1992).

Aviation Act (Ilmailulaki 1194/2009).

Bankruptcy Act (Konkurssilaki 120/2004).

Bonds or Promissory Notes Act (Velkakirjalaki 622/1947).

Building Protection Act (Rakennussuojelulaki 60/1985).

Business Mortgage Act (Yrityskiinnityslaki 634/1984).

Church Act (Kirkkolaki 1054/1993).

Act of Commerce (ComA, Kauppalaki 355/1987).

Commercial Code (ComC, Kauppakaari 1734).

Commercial Space Rent Act (Laki liikehuoneiston vuokrauksesta 482/1995).

Act on Common or Joint Areas (Yhteisaluelaki 758/1989).

Consumer Protection Act (Kuluttajansuojalaki 38/1978).

Contracts Act (Laki varallisuusoikeudellisista oikeustoimista 228/1929).

Property Conveyance Tax Act (Varainsiirtoverolaki 931/1996).

Copyright Act (Tekijänoikeuslaki 404/1961).

Donation (movable) Act (Lahjanlupauslaki 625/1947).

Act on Executive Enforcement (Ulosottokaari 705/2007.

Act on Environmental Impact Assessment (Laki ympäristövaikutusten arviointimenettelystä 468/1994).

Act on Environmental Liability (Ympäristövahinkolaki 737/1994).

Expropriation Act (ExprA, Laki kiinteän omaisuuden ja erityisten oikeuksien lunastamisesta 603/1977).

Farm Financial Aid Act (Maaseutuelinkeinojen rahoituslaki 329/1999).

Farm Subsidy Act (Laki tilatukijärjestelmän täytäntöönpanosta 557/2005).

Decree of the Council of State on the Enforcement of the CAP Farm Payment System (Valtioneuvoston asetus tilatukijärjestelmän täytäntöönpanosta 758/2005).
Foundation Act (Säätiölaki 109/1930).
Act on Freedom of Trade (Laki elinkeinon harjoittamisen oikeudesta 122/1919).
Group Claim Act (Ryhmäkannelaki 444/2007).
Act on Guardianship (Laki holhoustoimesta 442/1999).
Act on Habitation Right Flats (Laki asumisoikeusasunnoista 650/1990).
Habitation Sales Act (Asuntokauppalaki 843/1994).
Habitation Share Company Act (Asunto-osakeyhtiölaki 1599/2009).
Habitation Rent Act (Laki asuinhuoneiston vuokrauksesta 481/1995).
Heritage Code (HerC, Perintökaari 40/1965).Insurance Company Act (Vakuutusyhtiölaki 521/2008)
Instalment Purchase Act (Osamaksukauppalaki 91/1966).
Interest Act (Korkolaki 633/1982).
Act on Joint Ownership (Laki eräistä yhteisomistussuhteista 180/1958).
Code of Judicial Procedure (Oikeudenkäymiskaari 4/1734).
Land Register Act (Kiinteistörekisterilaki 392/1985).
Land Tenancy Act (Maanvuokralaki 258/1966).
Land Use (Planning) and Building Act (LUBA, Maankäyttö- ja rakennuslaki 132/1999).
Limitation Act (Laki velan vanhentumisesta 728/2003).
Lost Property Act (Löytötavaralaki 778/1988).
Marriage Act (Avioliittolaki 234/1929).
Mining Act (Kaivoslaki 621/2011).
Municipalities Act (Kuntalaki 365/1995).
Neighbourhood Relations Act (Laki eräistä naapuruussuhteista 26/1960).
Act on Notaries (Kaupanvahvistajalaki 573/2009).
Patent Act (Patenttilaki 550/1967).
Personal Data Act (Henkilörekisterilaki 523/1999).
Plant Breeding Rights Act (Laki kasvinjalostajanoikeudesta 1279/2009).
Pre-emption Act (Etuostolaki 608/1977).
Public Roads Act (Maantielaki 503/2005).
Private Roads Act (Laki yksityisistä teistä 358/1962).
Railways (Traffic) Act (Rautatielaki 304/2011).
Railways (Track) Act (Ratalaki 110/2007).
Real Estate Code (REC, Maakaari 540/1995).
(Old) Real Estate Code 1734 (Maakaari 31.12.1734).
Real Estate Formation Act (REFA, Kiinteistönmuodostamislaki 554/1995).Act on the Property Registration Reform (Laki kirjaamisasioiden siirtämistä koskevan lainsäädännön voimaanpanosta 584/2009).
Act on Recovery to Bankrupt's Estate (Laki takaisinsaannista konkurssipesään 758/1991).
Soil Excavation Act (Maa-aineslaki 555/1981).
Act on the State Council (Laki valtioneuvostosta 175/2003).
Act on the Surveillance of Foreign Purchase of Land (Laki ulkomailla asuvien ja ulkomaisten yhteisöjen kiinteistönhankintojen valvonnasta 1613/1992).
Trade Mark Act (Tavaramerkkilaki 7/1964).

Utility Models Act (Hyödyllisyysmallilaki 800/1991).
Vehicle Mortgage Act (Autokiinnityslaki 810/1972).
Vessel Mortgage Act (Aluskiinnityslaki 211/1927).
Water Act (Vesilaki 587/2011).

§2. CASE LAW SURVEYS

I. General

Finlex Data Bank; legislation and case law <www.finlex.fi/en>.

Decisions of the Supreme Court (Yearbook: Korkeimman oikeuden ratkaisuja, KKO).

Decisions of the Supreme Administrative Court (Yearbook: Korkeimman hallinto-oikeuden ratkaisuja, KHO).

II. Court Judgments and Decisions

Supreme Court (korkein oikeus, KKO):

1937 II 352	No.	470
1938 II 158		368
1953 II 19		468
1959 I 1		328
1965 II 57		325
1972 II 25		328
1984 II 223		517
1985 II 131		363
1992: 57		363
1997:210		137
1998: 131		584
1999: 92		535
1999:128		136
2003:2		181
2004:8		522
2005: 42		42
2007:25		593
2010:17		399a
2010:35		96
2011:62		597

Supreme Administrative Court (korkein hallinto-oikeus, KHO)

Selected Bibliography and Legal Sources

Index

The numbers here refer to paragraph numbers.

Index

www.ingramcontent.com/pod-product-compliance
Lightning Source LLC
Chambersburg PA
CBHW071446230926
51846CB00001B/357